The New World Order

Russell Burrill

Seminars Unlimited
P.O. Box 66
Keene, TX 76059

Edited by Ken McFarland
Cover design by Ed Guthero
Cover illustration by Darrel Tank

ISBN: 1-882704-00-2

Contents

About the Author

Russell Burrill is the Director of the North American Division Evangelism Institute in Chicago, Illinois. He has served not only as a pastor and evangelist in many parts of the United States, but is also in great demand as a speaker and trainer—having shared his insights into the prophecies of Daniel and Revelation with thousands across North America.

Russell is also the author of the popular Prophecy Seminar, attended by thousands across the United States, Canada, and overseas countries. This volume is the result of many requests to put into book form some of the material presented in these prophectic seminars.

Acknowledgments

The author would like to acknowledge many people who have helped in the preparation of this book—especially those who read the manuscript and offered suggestions for improvement.

Special thanks are also due to the author's secretary, Mrs. Genevieve Clark—and to the author's wife, Cynthia Burrill, for helping in preparation of the manuscript.

In addition, the author wishes to thank Carl Johnston, Director of Seminars Unlimited, for the many hours he spent in seeing this book through to completion. Countless other people also influenced its preparation, and to them all, the author is deeply indebted.

It is the prayer of the author that God will use this book to help prepare a people for the soon coming of our Lord Jesus Christ. As the book plainly reveals, we are currently living in the closing days of earth's history. World events are shaping up for the final countdown of the ages. This book is written not only to alert us to rapidly unfolding last-day events, but also to motivate people to prepare themselves for the greatest last-day event of them all—the return of Jesus to take us all home. Even so, come, Lord Jesus.

Foreword by
Mark Finley

Occasionally a book comes along which is must reading. I consider *The New World Order*, by Russell Burrill, such a book. It clearly reveals what's behind the rapid pace of change in our hectic world. It pulls the curtain aside, viewing geo-political events through the eyes of prophecy. It presents a sensible, carefully thought through, biblical approach to events now facing our world.

The New World Order reveals insights from the prophetic books of Daniel and Revelation which graphically illuminate the fall of communism, the rise of Catholicism, and the destination toward which the New World Order is heading.

Ours is a shaky world. For many, its future is

uncertain. Thousands look out over the horizon of the future, asking, "Where is this world headed? What does the future hold?" Russell Burrill's gripping analysis provides real hope for our time. He presents the only sensible answer to our current dilemma—the return of our Lord. Reading this volume, your heart will beat with a new determination to be ready for Jesus' coming. You will feel yourself drawn to your knees. It is my prayer that as you read these inspiring pages, you will be inspired with hope for the future. May your heart beat anew with the eager anticipation that soon—and very soon—we shall see the King.

Mark A Finley
Speaker
It Is Written Telecast

1

The New World Order

Rip Van Winkle, according to the famous story, fell asleep and woke up twenty years later to find that his little town had greatly changed. Imagine someone sleeping for twenty years and waking up today! The changes would be astronomical!

Twenty years ago the Soviet Union and the United States were locked in the midst of a cold war that sent shivers racing over the spines of countless thousands. The prospect of nuclear war seemed high. The United States was embroiled in a no-win contest in Vietnam, people were demonstrating in the streets against the war, and America was about to suffer the worst defeat in its history. Many were suggesting that America's leadership in world affairs was a relic of the past and that we were now living in America's declining years.

Yet Bible prophecy predicts—as we shall see later in this book—that America will be one of the leading participants in the closing scenes of earth's history. This seemed impossible twenty years ago, with American influence declining in the world. However, all that has now changed. We have entered a "new world order," as world leaders describe today's world.

Just think of what has transpired over the last twenty years, and the accelerating pace of change that has occurred in the last few years alone. The rate of change has been overwhelming. Each evening's newscast reveals another amazing development in our complex world.

In the last twenty years the world has gone through the agony of defeat in Vietnam, stood aghast at the killing fields of Cambodia, and been sickened by the attempted extermination of the Hmong people in Southeast Asia. We have witnessed the humiliating resignation of a president over Watergate and suffered the aftermath of distrust in leadership that followed. Just when we thought we had recovered, America was further humiliated by the detention of hostages in Iran. America seemed powerless to do anything to release them. It appeared that any country could humiliate the United States. Conditions didn't appear promising for the fulfillment of Revelation 13 any time soon.

Who could have predicted that in one decade, America's prospects could change from humiliation to glory? Yet they have. In 1980 Ronald Reagan was elected president of the United States. Reagan inspired hope in Americans once again, despite the fact that many disagreed with his policies. America began to take pride in itself. Many subtle changes during these years led America once again to the forefront of world power. Reagan initiated one of the largest peacetime military buildups ever. America rescued the tiny island of Grenada in the Caribbean from communist control. That appeared to be a turning point.

In the aftermath of Grenada, America gained a new respect in the world—a respect it had lost in Vietnam and Iran. Communism, which had seemed to be expanding in the early 80s with increasing strength, was suddenly halted in the Western Hemisphere. People began to feel that America was once again a force to be reckoned with.

It wasn't long before other changes in America's leadership began to be noticed. The Soviet Union and the United States for the first time sat down and seriously began to discuss nuclear disarmament. Not only did they discuss it, but in the end they actually voted to begin disarmament. These meetings in Iceland were the beginning of the end of the Cold War.

The election of Gorbachev in the Soviet Union signaled the beginning of other enormous changes for our world. For the first time, the "evil empire," as Reagan called the Soviet Union, was opening up to new ideas. "Perestroika" began to open doors that had seemed impenetrable in previous administrations. This paved the way for the shaking of the communist empire around the world. Overnight, it seemed, communism disappeared.

The collapse of communism raced like a tidal wave across the world. Nothing could stop it. One of the greatest revolutions in human history has occurred in the last few years, and it has been virtually bloodless. Like falling dominos, the eastern bloc countries of Poland, East Germany, Czechoslovakia, Romania, Bulgaria, Hungary, and Albania expunged communism.

The revolution that rocked communist Europe soon swept into the Soviet Union, which seemed on the verge of collapse. No longer were Soviet citizens content with the ways of the past. Freedom was reborn. Once they had tasted liberty, nothing could send them back to totalitarianism. The failed coup in August of 1991 placed the final nail in the coffin of the Soviet Union. The old union was dead, and the new commonwealth was born. Gorbachev resigned, and the Soviet Union was disbanded— all with very little bloodshed. The United States emerged as the great superpower in the world, a unique and unprecedented position in world affairs.

Twenty years ago no one paid much attention to what America said. Even the United Nations did little to make America feel it was a major power in world affairs. In fact, the United Nations often seemed more concerned with humiliating the United States than following its lead.

Then in August of 1990 the world was stunned when Iraq invaded the little country of Kuwait and attempted to annex it. The resulting events have had a major impact on the role of the United States in world affairs. Other nations have periodically invaded other countries, and no one seems to have noticed. But something happened with "Operation Desert Storm" that propelled the United States into a new position of world leadership, its wishes honored and respected around the world.

As George Bush led the United States in "Operation Desert Storm," he did something no other United States president had ever done. Rather than just commit the troops of America to Kuwait, Bush garnered the support of the entire world community. For the first time in the modern era, nearly all the nations of the earth joined together against another power. George Bush, leading America, accomplished this, and the United Nations followed America's lead. Everything America did in the Persian Gulf was accomplished under the authority of the United Nations. Never before has there been such common unity for a major undertaking among the diverse nations of earth. Kuwait marked the beginning of the new world order, with America in charge.

In the aftermath of the Kuwait liberation, the United States has suddenly emerged as the world power to contend with. Small nations that were aligned with the communist bloc have become surprisingly cooperative, recognizing the new situation that exists in a world with only one superpower. For the first time in history, this reality dawned when Israelis and Arabs sat down at the negotiating table and actually began to talk with each other. This is the new world order—and America is in the lead.

On January 28, 1992, George Bush, in his State of the Union address to the Congress of the United

States, officially declared the end of the Cold War. But that long chill in superpower relations was not just at an end—the fact is that the United States *won* the Cold War. We are indeed living in a new world order.

Not only have we entered a new political world order, but also a religious one. The United States, from its inception, has been a land where individual liberties were cherished and protected. But shockingly, the scenario of last-day events revealed in the Book of Revelation anticipates a yet-future time when those liberties—so long cherished in freedom-loving America—will disappear, with religious intolerance taking their place.

Changes negatively affecting religious liberty and the separation of church and state have been occurring steadily over the last several years. This too may be paving the way for a new world order in which liberty of conscience will no longer be respected. During the Reagan years, the United States for the first time recognized the Vatican as a separate government by sending an ambassador to that religious province. According to *U. S. News and World Report* (August 13, 1990), George Bush and Pope John Paul II discussed world affairs on the telephone at least once a week. It is fascinating that in the new world order that has arisen, the president of the United States and the head of the largest Christian church in the world can be in weekly contact to discuss world affairs. Perhaps the religion of the Vatican is having a greater impact on America than many realize.

During the Reagan-Bush years, we have seen a new Supreme Court appointed—a much more conservative Supreme Court—and one many feel may erode some of the cherished freedoms gained in previous courts, particularly those freedoms associated with the separation of church and state.

At the same time, the religious right has increased its influence in American political life. From Jerry Falwell's "Moral Majority" to Pat Robertson's run for the presidency, the religious right is exercising an ever-increasing role in America and in its influence on the White House. We will examine more of these issues later on in this book.

What does all of this mean? What about the new world order that has resulted from the United States becoming the one and only world superpower? This power, nearly all nations of the world now respect and follow. Even more interesting, it is a power that at this time seems to be influenced by two major religious forces: the Vatican and the religious right—two entities that seem worlds apart, but whose goals may be very similar.

It seems apparent that the world may well be gearing up for the final fulfillment of Revelation, chapter 13. Never in the history of the United States have all the events described there seemed so possible of fulfillment as at the present. Of course, only time will verify what will happen, but certainly these events call for a new study of the prophecies of Daniel and Revelation, in view of the gigantic changes that have recently occurred on our battered planet.

In order to comprehend the magnitude of what is now transpiring on Planet Earth, we wish to study the prophecies of Daniel and Revelation in a new light. We will take a quick look at the prophecies of Daniel, chapters 2 and 7, and then move into an understanding of Daniel 11. We will spend most of our time in this book unraveling the tremendous prophecies of this chapter, which provides insights into some of the climactic changes that have so rapidly occurred in our world. We will then center our attention on Revelation 13 and 16, where all the prophecies of Daniel find their ultimate fulfillment. The final chapter in this book will explain what this all means to us today. So get ready for a fantastic adventure in understanding Bible prophecy in light of the tremendous changes currently taking place in our world!

2

Unraveling Daniel's Mystic Symbols

Have you ever put together a puzzle? Some of them can be very challenging. Just when you think you have the right piece for a certain part of the puzzle, you discover it doesn't quite fit. You even try to force it a little, and at times it seemingly goes into place. Later on, however, you find it fits better somewhere else. Daniel's prophecies sometimes seem like a gigantic jigsaw puzzle. When we have the right interpretation, all the pieces come together perfectly. In our humanity, we sometimes try to force some of the pieces, until we inevitably see God's perfect picture.

In attempting to understand Daniel's prophecies, we must ever keep in mind our humanity. When dealing with prophecies yet to be fulfilled, there always must be some tentativeness in our conclusions. We have not yet seen God's perfect picture. However, God is permitting us to see how the big pieces fit together. Most problems in interpreting Daniel and Revelation occur because we try to figure out too many of the details, instead of beholding the larger picture God is drawing for us. Thankfully, the interpretation becomes clear when the prophecy is fulfilled, for all the pieces of the puzzle now fit together perfectly.

Chapters 2 and 7 have been the best understood of all the chapters in the Book of the Daniel. But Daniel 11 has mystified Bible readers for centuries. Some of the chapter's fulfillment is still in the future, rather than having primarily transpired in the past, such as with Daniel 2 and 7. This has created uncertainty in understanding Daniel 11. As we examine this chapter in great detail, we want to keep in mind that our conclusions are always tentative, waiting until their fulfillment thoroughly vindicates them. However, recent events give credence to the interpretation taken in this book. At least in the big picture, the exciting news is that we might well be on track in our understanding of this incredible prophecy.

Ways to Interpret Prophecy

In our day there are three schools of interpretation for the prophecies of Daniel and Revelation. The *preterist* position attempts to explain the prophecies of Daniel and Revelation as already fulfilled in the past. For example, Daniel's prophecy of the little horn in Daniel 8 is viewed as the invasion of the Jewish Temple by Antiochus Epiphanes in the second century B.C. The basic philosophy behind this method of interpretation seems to be that Daniel was written *after* the event, and the prophecy is treated as if it were merely recorded history. This seems to be a basic denial of the inspiration of Scripture and is totally rejected in this book.

The second school of interpretation, known as *futurism*, has become fairly popular in the last several years. Futurism teaches that the fulfillment of most of the prophecies in Daniel and Revelation is still future. For futurists, the antichrist is not a system that ruled the world for many centuries, but is seen rather as an individual who will rule the world in the future. Since this system of interpretation does not anchor the prophecy to a historical event in the prophet's time, it is strongly influenced by world events. Advocates of this view championed Saddam Hussein's invasion of Kuwait as a fulfillment of Bible prophecy. They compared him to ancient Nebuchadnezzar. Subsequent events, of course, proved them wrong. But that fails to stop them from using prophecy to guess what is coming next. This view becomes highly speculative. The eventual result of this method is to create a disbelief in Scripture, since its advocates keep changing interpretation as events unfold. Because of the speculative, fanciful nature of this method of interpretation, it is also totally rejected in this book.

The third school of interpretation is called *historicism*. This method of interpretation believes that prophecy continually unfolds as history advances. It sees the prophecies of Daniel and Revelation beginning in the prophet's time and continuing until the time of the end. In this way, one can trace the unfolding of Bible prophecy through the ages. One can see what has transpired already, where we are now, and what is yet to come. This method of interpretation seems to be validated by the prophet Daniel himself as he gives the interpretation of Daniel 2 and 7. It has been the traditional interpretation of the Christian church from its earliest centuries. It was the method of interpreting the prophecies used by Luther and other great Reformers. Futurism and preterism have only existed in the last few hundred years. They originated in the Catholic counter-reformation in the sixteenth century. These methods of interpretation have only become popular in the last 100 years.

Another feature of historicism is that the prophecies of Daniel build on each other. In other words, Daniel 2 gives us the grand outline of world history, Daniel 7 adds further details, Daniel 8 and 9 still more details, and Daniel 11 goes over the same ground with even greater detail. We will discover that each prophecy expands our understanding of the end times, by introducing a new power or event that is only hinted at in the previous prophecy. Furthermore, we will discover that the part expanded in Daniel 7 and 11 is further expanded in Revelation. We must not miss that connection.

Because this method of interpretation is validated by the Book of Daniel itself, because it has been the historical interpretation of the Christian Church from its inception, and because this method of interpretation has stood the test of time and has been validated by the events of history, this book accepts this school of interpretation as the correct way to understand the books of Daniel and Revelation. It is this method that will be used exclusively in this book.

The Great Image

Daniel's first prophetic scenario unfolds through an impressive dream that the Babylonian king, Nebuchadnezzar, received from the God of heaven. This fascinating dream depicted a great image composed of various metals, representing the various empires that would arise from Nebuchadnezzar's day onward. The head of the image was gold, the breast and arms were silver, the belly and thighs were brass, the legs were iron, and the feet were iron and clay. An immense stone of gigantic proportions plummeted from heaven, crushed the image's feet, and ground the image to powder:

> Thou, O king, sawest, and behold a great image. This great image, whose brightness was excellent, stood before thee; and the form thereof was terrible. This image's head was of fine gold, his breast and his arms of silver, his belly and his thighs of brass, his legs of iron, his feet part of iron and part of clay. Thou sawest till that a stone was cut out without hands, which smote the image upon his feet that were of iron and clay, and brake them to pieces. Then was the iron, the clay, the brass, the silver, and the gold, broken to pieces together, and became like the chaff of the summer threshingfloors; and the wind carried them away, that no place was found for them: and the stone that smote the image became a

great mountain, and filled the whole earth.
(Daniel 2:31-35.)

The critical part of Daniel's recitation in chapter 2 is the fact that he not only portrays this remarkable prophecy to the king, but gives us the interpretation as well. "This is the dream; and we will tell the interpretation thereof before the king" (Daniel 2:36). Daniel's interpretation of this image is the basis upon which we have accepted the historical method of interpretation.

Daniel clearly pinpoints Nebuchadnezzar's Babylon as the head of gold:

> Thou, O king, art a king of kings: for the God of heaven hath given thee a kingdom, power, and strength, and glory. And wheresoever the children of men dwell, the beasts of the field and the fowls of the heaven hath he given into thine hand, and hath made thee ruler over them all. Thou art this head of gold. (Daniel 2:37, 38).

The prophecy begins in the prophet's day, but Daniel illuminates the future by stating that other kingdoms will follow Babylon. Just as silver was inferior to gold, so the kingdom that followed Babylon—the kingdom of the Medes and Persians—would be inferior to Babylon: "And after thee shall arise another kingdom inferior to thee, and another third kingdom of brass, which shall bear rule over all the earth" (Daniel 2:39). The third kingdom of brass—Greece—would follow in rapid succession. Finally, the iron monarchy of Rome would rule over the world: "And the fourth kingdom shall be strong as iron: forasmuch as iron breaketh in pieces and subdueth all things: and as iron that breaketh all these, shall it break in pieces and bruise" (Daniel 2:40). Yet even Rome's iron hand would not last forever. Eventually the kingdom would be divided and would become as weak as iron and clay mixed together:

> And whereas thou sawest the feet and toes, part of potters' clay, and part of iron, the kingdom shall be divided; but there shall be in it of the strength of the iron, forasmuch as thou sawest the iron mixed with miry clay. And as the toes of the feet were part of iron, and part of clay, so the kingdom shall be partly strong, and partly broken. And whereas thou sawest iron mixed with miry clay, they shall mingle themselves with the seed of men: but they shall not cleave one to another, even as iron is not mixed with clay. (Verses 41-43.)

Any student of world history quickly sees how impressively Daniel has portrayed world history hundreds of years in advance. The four great empires of antiquity appeared exactly as foretold. While there were other great empires in the ancient world, these four are highlighted because they were the powers that affected God's ancient people, Israel. The biblical prophecies always seem to zero in on powers that affect God's covenant people.

Since the breakup of the Roman empire in A.D. 476, the European continent has remained in a divided state, exactly as Daniel foretold. People have tried to unite the various powers through marriage alliances, military conquests, and economic pressure, but all have failed. So declares the prophecy: "And whereas thou sawest iron mixed with miry clay, they shall mingle themselves with the seed of men: but they shall not cleave one to another, even as iron is not mixed with clay" (Daniel 2:43). It should be noted that Revelation does point to a short time just before Christ comes when all the world will again be reunited against the covenant people (Revelation 17:12-14).

One final event emerges at the end of Daniel's first prophecy: a great stone, cut out without human hands, which crashes to the earth and destroys the image. This great stone symbolizes God's kingdom:

> And in the days of these kings shall the God of heaven set up a kingdom, which shall never be destroyed: and the kingdom shall not be left to other people, but it shall break in pieces and consume all these kingdoms, and it shall stand for ever. (Daniel 2:44.)

This kingdom will not take over earthly kingdoms, but will completely subdue and destroy them. Here Daniel gives us the focal point of his prophecies—the establishment of God's eternal kingdom that will never be destroyed. The good news of the prophecies of Daniel is that the God of heaven will set up this kingdom. This is the event to which all prophecy points.

In this first prophetic vision of Daniel, God has given us the basic principle to interpret his prophecies. Note how the prophecy begins in Daniel's day, gradually unfolds in great epochal events down through history, and climaxes with the establishment of God's kingdom. All future prophecies of Daniel will follow this same sequence, but each will elaborate, not only each area of the prophecy, but particularly the time just before the final climax of history.

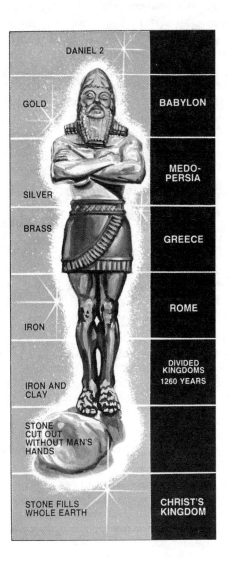

DANIEL 2

GOLD — BABYLON

SILVER — MEDO-PERSIA

BRASS — GREECE

IRON — ROME

IRON AND CLAY — DIVIDED KINGDOMS 1260 YEARS

STONE CUT OUT WITHOUT MAN'S HANDS

STONE FILLS WHOLE EARTH — CHRIST'S KINGDOM

Our purpose in reviewing Daniel 2 and 7 is not to give a detailed exposition. It is assumed that the reader of this book is already familiar with these basic prophecies. Our focus will be Daniel 11, that final great prophetic chapter. Our review of these two chapters is merely to help us gain the perspective for our interpretation of Daniel 11. Only as we understand these two chapters will we be prepared to unravel the tremendous revelation of Daniel 11.

The Panorama of the Beasts

In Daniel 7 the imagery changes, but the interpretation is the same as for Daniel 2. Instead of four metals, four beasts symbolize the various nations that will affect the covenant people. "The four great beasts are four kingdoms that will rise from the earth" (Daniel 7:17, NIV).

The first of these beasts was the lion with eagle's wings, representing the empire of Babylon. As in Daniel 2, the prophecy begins with the current empire of Daniel's day:

> The first was like a lion, and had eagle's wings: I beheld till the wings thereof were plucked, and it was lifted up from the earth, and made stand upon the feet as a man, and a man's heart was given to it. (Daniel 7:4.)

Very quickly Daniel is shown another beast—a bear—representing the next great empire to affect God's covenant people—Medeo-Persia:

> And behold another beast, a second, like to a bear, and it raised up itself on one side, and it had three ribs in the mouth of it between the teeth of it: and they said thus unto it, Arise, devour much flesh. (Daniel 7:5.)

Daniel's next beast is the leopard-like beast with four heads, representing the great empire of Greece:

> After this I beheld, and lo another, like a leopard, which had upon the back of it four wings of a fowl: the beast had also four heads; and dominion was given to it. (Daniel 7:6.)

Alexander the Great led the Greeks in conquest of the Persians in the battle of Arbella in 331 B.C. Yet Alexander soon died in a drunken brawl. His kingdom was quickly divided among his four generals and became the kingdoms of Egypt, Thrace, Macedonia, and Syria. Accurately, Daniel had predicted both the rise and division of the Grecian empire.

> After this I saw in the night visions, and behold a fourth beast, dreadful and terrible, and strong exceedingly; and it had great iron teeth: it devoured and brake in pieces, and stamped the residue with the feet of it: and it was diverse from all the beasts that were before it; and it had ten horns. (Daniel 7:7.)

As in Daniel 2, the fourth empire that followed Greece was Rome. Similarity is seen between the two symbols in the mention of the legs of iron in Daniel 2 and the teeth of iron in Chapter 7. Likewise, Daniel 7 does not portray another power conquering Rome. Instead, it predicts a division of the Roman empire. True to the prediction, the power of Rome was broken in A.D. 476 by the invasion of Germanic tribes into the Roman empire. In the aftermath of this invasion, Rome was divided into ten parts—the ten horns of the vision:

"The ten horns are ten kings who shall arise from this kingdom" (Daniel 7:24, NKJV).

With unerring accuracy Daniel has traced world history again, demonstrating a remarkable understanding of the various empires to arise and supplying detailed information about them. Daniel 7 has further verified the historical method of interpretation.

The Little Horn

However, the purpose of Daniel 7 is not just to restate the prophecy of Daniel 2 with a few further details. Rather, the recitation of the empires gives the historical setting for the new power that Daniel introduces in chapter seven—the little horn. The little horn power which becomes the focus of Daniel 7 cannot be understood apart from its historical context.

Who is this little horn that arises in the midst of the Roman empire's divisions? Let's take the time to quickly enumerate what Daniel 7 reveals concerning this new power and then identify it. This identification is essential to a proper understanding of Daniel 11. Daniel 11 will go through the sequence of empires again, including the little horn, and then will add one final power that will seek to trample down the people of God at the end of time. Only by understanding Daniel's prophecy of the little horn can we hope to fully understand the final crisis that is coming to this world.

Open your Bible and follow along as Daniel unfolds for us various identification marks of the little horn power.

1. The little horn arose among the ten horns.

I considered the horns, and, behold, there came

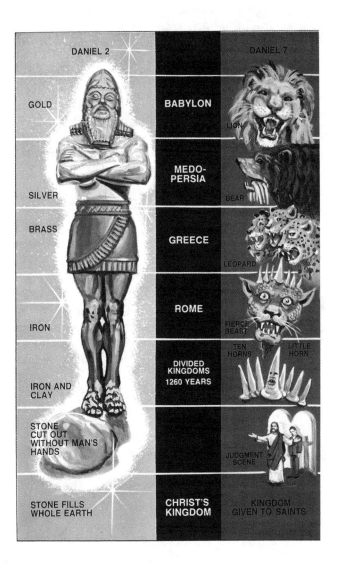

up among them another little horn. (Daniel 7:8.)

Since the little horn arose among the ten horns, we should look for this power to arise in Europe after the breakup of the Roman Empire in A.D. 476.

2. The little horn destroyed three horns.

". . . before whom there were three of the first horns plucked up by the roots" (verse 8).

Amazingly, only seven of the original ten divisions of the Roman Empire survived. Three disappeared from history. Daniel declared that the little horn power would be responsible.

3. The little horn had eyes like a man.

"In this horn were eyes like the eyes of man" (verse 8).

Evidently a man is at the head or in control of this power.

4. The little horn spoke boastfully and blasphemed.

". . . a mouth speaking great things" (verse 8). "And he shall speak great words against the Most High" (verse 25). There is a religious nature to the little horn. He not only does political things but is also involved in religion. Yet this involvement is blasphemous and seems to be one of the great crimes of this power. In Bible times, blasphemy was when a mere human being claimed the power to forgive sins (Mark 2:7) or when a man claimed the prerogatives of God (John 10:33). In either case, the little horn power engages in blasphemous activity.

5. The little horn power persecuted those who disagreed.

"and shall wear out the saints..." (Daniel 7:25).

Shockingly, those who disagreed with the monstrous claims of this power would suffer persecution.

6. The little horn would presumptuously think to change God's law and the times.

"... think to change times and laws" (Daniel 7:25).

Changing God's law is unthinkable, yet Daniel predicted that this political power would enter the religious arena by even attempting to change God's law.

7. The little horn would reign for a staggering 1260 years.

> "Then the saints shall be given into his hand for a time and times and half a time" (Daniel 7:25, NKJV).

The Book of Revelation enables us to unravel Daniel's symbolic language here. Revelation 13:4 refers to this time as 42 months. Forty-two months times 30 days in a month would equal 1260 days. Furthermore, Revelation 12:14 refers to this period as a time, times, and half a time, while verse 6 of the same chapter specifically calls it 1260 days. By comparing these, it is obvious that Daniel is referring to a period of 1260 days. Since a day is symbolic of one year in biblical time prophecy (Ezekiel 4:6), 1260 days would equate with 1260 literal years that the little horn power would exercise dominion over the saints of God.

These seven identification marks of the little horn make it crystal clear that Daniel is describing the Christian church during the Dark Ages. During this time the church indeed took on the characteristics of intolerance and persecution, uniting with the state to enforce its decrees. While the Roman Church was the primary power in control of the church during this period, it is not the only one here included.

Even after the Protestant Reformation began, intolerance and persecution continued. Protestants arranged for the state to support their religion and enforced it by law. Daniel 7, in its historical context, refers primarily to this sad chapter in the history of the church when persecution and intolerance marked its existence. During this time there were sincere and good people both in the little horn system and outside it. Daniel is not attacking people in this chapter, but a system that ended up keeping people from fully understanding the God of heaven.

Please note how the church of the Dark Ages fulfills each of Daniel's marks of identification.

1. It arose among the ten divisions. As the Roman Empire disintegrated, another power emerged as the unifying power among all the ten divisions of the Roman Empire. That power was the bishop of Rome. No other such power arose among the ten divisions of the Roman Empire at that time.

2. It plucked up three horns. As the bishop of Rome surfaced among the ten divisions of the Roman Empire, there were three powers that refused to submit to his authority. They were the Heruli, the Vandals, and the Ostrogoths. To achieve full unity, the church encouraged armies to destroy these three powers. The last one was destroyed in A.D. 538. No other power arose at the time so clearly specified in the prophecy as did the medieval papacy.

3. It had eyes like a man. Indeed, a man appeared

at the head of the church during this time, exercising universal power and dominion.

4. It was a blasphemous power. As the medieval church gained power and ascendancy, it made very boastful and blasphemous claims. Just as blasphemy in Bible times was to claim to forgive sins and to claim to have the power of God, so the medieval church made similar claims.

> And God himself is obliged to abide by the judgment of his priests, and either not to pardon or to pardon, according as they refuse to give absolution, provided the penitent is capable of it.—*Dignity and Duties of the Priest,* by Liguori, p. 27.

> Hence priests are called the parents of Jesus Christ: such is the title that St. Bernard gives them, for they are the active cause by which he is made to exist really in the consecrated Host.

> Thus the priest may, in a certain manner, be called the creator of his Creator, since by saying the words of consecration, he creates, as it were, Jesus in the sacrament.—*Dignity and Duties of the Priest,* by Liguori, p. 32.

> Thou art the shepherd, thou art the physician, thou art the director, thou art the husbandman; finally, thou art another god on earth.—From the oration of Christopher Marcellus in the fourth session of the Fifth Lateran Council in 1512, addressing the Pope. Labbe and Gossard, *History of Councils.* Vol. 14, col. 109.

Not only did the medieval church make these very boastful and blasphemous claims, but it also introduced many changes into Christianity directly from paganism:

> We are told in various ways by Eusebius, that

Constantine, in order to recommend the new religion to the heathen, transferred into it the outward ornaments to which they had been accustomed in their own. It is not necessary to go into a subject which the diligence of Protestant writers has made familiar to most of us. The use of temples, and these dedicated to particular saints, and ornamented on occasions with branches of trees, incense, lamps, and candles; votive offerings on recovery from illness, holy water; asylums; holydays and seasons, use of calendars, processions, blessings on the fields; sacerdotal vestments; the tonsure, the ring in marriage, turning to the East, images at a later date, perhaps the ecclesiastical chant, and the Kyrie Eleisen, are all of pagan origin, and sanctified by their adoption into the Church.—John Henry Cardinal Newman, *An Essay on the Development of Christian Doctrine,* Longmans, Green & Company, London, 1920, p. 373.

5. **It persecuted those who disagreed with its claims.** This period of church history, as well as world history, is noted for its totalitarianism and persecution of dissenters. Over 50 million people died for their faith during this terrible time of persecution. Romanists killed heretics and Protestants, and Protestants killed Catholics as well as other Protestants. Whatever religion gained control of the political power used that power against dissenters. While many Protestants claimed to have left medieval Catholicism, history indicates that most of them continued in the ways of Romanism by uniting church and state.

6. **He thinks that he has changed the law of God.** Changing God's law is unthinkable. Yet strangely, the medieval church thought its power so great

that it would actually attempt to change the very law of God. So during this time, great changes took place in the church: pagan practices were substituted for those enjoined by the Bible and even the Ten Commandments. The Ten Commandments were altered to allow for image worship, worship was sanctified on the first day instead of the seventh as commanded by God, and pagan practices and holy days were enjoined upon the people.

7. This state of things continued for exactly 1260 years. The medieval papacy ascended to full religious and political power in A.D. 538, when the decree of the Emperor Justinian took effect, granting the Roman pontiff full power in the West. While the decree was issued in A.D. 533, it did not go into full force until five years later when the last of the three Arian heretical powers were put out of the way.

Twelve hundred and sixty years later, in A.D. 1798, the French general Berthier, under Napoleon, entered the Vatican, took the Pope prisoner, and ended the political power of the medieval papacy. The political power of the church was thus broken, and persecution ebbed. This political downfall of the papacy affected both Catholics and Protestants. As a result, religious intolerance began to ebb, especially with the ensuing development of religious liberty in America.

These seven identifying marks make it very clear that the medieval church—which included both Catholics and Protestants and that greatly persecuted those who disagreed with it—is Daniel's little horn. This does not mean that all who belonged to the system were evil; they were not.

What Daniel predicts is that corruption would infiltrate the church. Both Catholics and Protestants today abhor what happened to the church during this time of deep apostasy.

However, let us not just dismiss this as a history lesson, for we will discover in another chapter that Daniel's little horn is similar to another period of religious intolerance coming in the future. While Daniel 7 focuses our attention on the medieval church, Daniel 11 and Revelation 13 will focus our attention on religious intolerance at the time of the end.

Our purpose in this chapter has been to trace the sequence of the unfolding events predicted in the Book of Daniel. Daniel 2 and 7 portray the same sequence of empires. Daniel 7 covers the same ground as Daniel 2, but with significant additions; namely, the little horn. This sequence is repeated again in Daniel 11, but this time Daniel will focus on the final great oppressor of God's people. That will be the subject of the rest of this book. Remember the sequence: Babylon, Media-Persia, Greece, Rome, 10 divisions of Europe, the medieval church. And then the focal point of it all: the day when the Ancient of Days will sit and the kingdoms of this world become the kingdoms of our Christ.

> But the saints of the most High shall take the kingdom, and possess the kingdom for ever, even for ever and ever. (Daniel 7:18.)

> And the kingdom and dominion, and the greatness of the kingdom under the whole heaven, shall be given to the people of the saints of the most High, whose kingdom is an everlasting

kingdom, and all dominions shall serve and obey him. (Daniel 7:27.)

May that day dawn soon!

3

The Eleventh of Daniel

Symbols! The Book of Daniel is full of them. The great image in Daniel 2 symbolized coming empires. The four separate beasts in Daniel 7 portrayed the nations that were to arise in opposition to the covenant people. Now Daniel 11 traces the same historical period with different symbols: the king of the north and the king of the south. Interestingly, in Daniel 11 the symbol is constant, but the meaning varies. What is Daniel's message through this final symbol? Different nations are to arise, but one power is behind them all—Satan himself.

Amazingly, Daniel draws aside the curtain and reveals to us that behind all the attempts of nations to destroy the covenant people of God is the same usurper—Satan. Once again Daniel portrays the great controversy theme that is the foundation for understanding the Book of Daniel.

In this chapter we will explore the same sequence we found in Daniel 2 and 7. Our purpose here is to discover the context for the final power that seeks to destroy the covenant people. This will be examined in Daniel 11:40-45. First, notice the sequence of empires that leads up to verses 40-45:

> And now will I shew thee the truth. Behold, there shall stand up yet three kings in Persia; and the fourth shall be far richer than they all: and by his strength through his riches he shall stir up all against the realm of Grecia. (Daniel 11:2.)

The 11th chapter of Daniel was written during the first year of the Medo-Persian empire (Daniel 11:1). Since Babylon has already faded into ancient history, there is no need to begin the prophecy in the Babylonian empire. Instead, Daniel commences this sequence with the Medo-Persian reign. The four kings mentioned above are Cambyses, False Smerdis, Darius, and Xerxes.

> And a mighty king shall stand up, that shall rule with great dominion, and do according to his will. And when he shall stand up, his kingdom shall be broken, and shall be divided toward the four winds of heaven; and not to his posterity, nor according to his dominion which he ruled: for his kingdom shall be plucked up, even for others beside those. (Daniel 11:3, 4.)

Daniel rapidly carries us through the sequence of empires. Brushing through the Medo-Persian rule in just one short verse, he quickly reveals the rise of Alexander the Great and the division of his empire to his four generals, rather than to heirs. The generals were: Lysimachus, Seleucus, Ptolemy, and Cassander. This portion of the prophecy corresponds exactly with the revelation in Daniel 7:6, which described Greece under the symbolism of a leopard with four heads.

Added details about the Grecian empire are then elaborated on in Daniel 11:5-15. Here the symbols of the king of the north and the king of the south are introduced, to portray the various divisions that occurred in the aftermath of the breakup of Alexander's empire.

Verses 16-30 describe the dominance of the king of the north, who evolves into the pagan Roman empire during these verses. Note that the symbol stays the same, but the nation represented by the symbol changes as time continues. Pagan Rome's activity is described by these verses:

> Then shall stand up in his estate a raiser of taxes in the glory of the kingdom: but within few days he shall be destroyed, neither in anger, nor in battle. (Verse 20.)

> And with the arms of a flood shall they be overflown from before him, and shall be broken; yea, also the prince of the covenant. (Verse 22.)

> Then shall he return into his land with great riches; and his heart shall be against the holy covenant; and he shall do exploits, and return to his own land. (Verse 28.)

The pagan Roman empire—the great taxer of the people—is symbolized, with verse 20 being a possible reference to Caesar Augustus. The prince of the covenant refers to Christ, whom the Roman empire nailed to a cross, as indicated in this prophecy. The Roman Empire's vicious attacks against Judaism and early Christianity are foretold in verse 28, as Rome becomes the great persecutor of God's people.

Daniel 11 travels the same outline of world history that we saw unfolded in Daniel 2 and 7. Daniel 11 again links us to the devastating effect of the church of the Dark Ages, as our knowledge of the little horn of Daniel 7 is enlarged. Now the little horn is also identified as the king of the north. This helps us understand that the power controlling even the church during this dark time of apostasy is the same power that controlled the Roman Empire. Even the Christian Church would be infiltrated by the devil himself. No more devastating attack could be launched against the disciples of Christ than an attack from within that first corrupted and then sought to destroy true discipleship. The great apostasy appears in Daniel 11 under the symbolism of the king of the north, in Daniel 11:31-39:

> And arms shall stand on his part, and they shall pollute the sanctuary of strength, and shall take away the daily sacrifice, and they shall place the abomination that maketh desolate. (Daniel 11:31.)

> And the king shall do according to his will; and he shall exalt himself, and magnify himself above every god, and shall speak marvellous things against the God of gods, and shall prosper till the indignation be accomplished: for that that is determined shall be done. (Daniel 11:36.)

Daniel pictures this apostate church of the Dark Ages desecrating God's temple by claiming to be the rightful heir to the Christian heritage, while at the same time destroying the essential elements of Christianity. Chapter 11 links us with chapter 7 in verse 36, as Daniel pictures this power speaking great things against God.

Daniel 11 has portrayed for us the same sequence of empires and powers that the other chapters in Daniel have predicted. The sequence is identical: Babylon, Medo-Persia, Greece, the divisions of Greece, pagan Rome, and the Church of the Dark Ages. All that the previous chapters have revealed is reviewed in these first 39 verses of chapter 11. Daniel 2 and 7, having covered these historical events quickly, point to the grand consummation of the ages. In Daniel 2, it is the stone kingdom that ushers in God's kingdom. In Daniel 7, the judgment sits and determines the destiny of those powers standing in opposition to God. However, in Daniel 11, after verse 39, we have an additional detailed description of last day events.

The Final King of the North

Daniel 11:39 brought us to A.D. 1798, the end of the 1260-year prophecy. This is the end of the time when the church dominates the state. Daniel 11:40 describes events transpiring at that time and then continues the description of the very end of human history. These next few verses will be the subject of the rest of our study, as we examine this final great king of the north that arises in opposition to the covenant people at the time of the end.

Note the revelation of this power which Daniel gives us:

> And at the time of the end shall the king of the south push at him: and the king of the north shall

come against him like a whirlwind, with chariots, and with horsemen, and with many ships; and he shall enter into the countries, and shall overflow and pass over. He shall enter also into the glorious land, and many countries shall be overthrown: but these shall escape out of his hand, even Edom, and Moab, and the chief of the children of Ammon. He shall stretch forth his hand also upon the countries: and the land of Egypt shall not escape. But he shall have power over treasures of gold and of silver, and over all the precious things of Egypt; and the Libyans and the Ethiopians shall be at his steps. But tidings out of the east and out of the north shall trouble him; therefore he shall go forth with great fury to destroy, and utterly to make away many. And he shall plant the tabernacles of his palace between the seas in the glorious holy mountain; yet he shall come to his end, and none shall help him.

And at that time shall Michael stand up, the great prince which standeth for the children of thy people: and there shall be a time of trouble, such as never was since there was a nation even to that same time: and at that time thy people shall be delivered, every one that shall be found written in the book. And many of them that sleep in the dust of the earth shall awake, some to everlasting life, and some to shame and everlasting contempt. And they that be wise shall shine as the brightness of the firmament; and they that turn many to righteousness as the stars for ever and ever. But thou, O Daniel, shut up the words, and seal the book, even to the time of the end: many shall run to and fro, and knowledge shall be increased. (Daniel 11:40-12:4.)

Here the final climax of human history is foretold. This last great power that rises against the people of God is defeated at the second coming of

Jesus. Then the dead rise, and God delivers His people. Here is foretold a final great time of trouble, in the midst of which God's people will be delivered. That's the good news that is the climax of the Book of Daniel. We know the outcome. Victory is sure for the people of the covenant.

As we glance at the above crucial passage, it becomes clear that if we are to understand it, we will need first to understand the symbols employed. There are three basic symbols we will seek to interpret in the next three chapters:

1. The glorious holy mountain. What is this mountain that the king of the north attempts to conquer? For it is the glorious holy mountain that becomes the focal point of the king of the north's attack in the final hour. We must identify this symbol.

2. The king of the north. This symbol has changed since it first referred to one of the divisions of the Grecian empire. Who then is this final king of the north, who makes the final attack against the holy people?

3. The king of the south. This symbol disappeared from the chapter while the church was in apostasy. Now it reappears in verse 40 with a vicious attack against the king of the north at the time of the end. But then the king of the north counterattacks and destroys the king of the south. Who is this king of the south?

Once we have made these identifications, we will return to Daniel 11:40-45 and discover an exciting fulfillment of this prophecy, possibly in the process of being fulfilled today in the new world order.

4

The Glorious Holy Mountain

A nd he shall plant the tabernacle of his palace between the seas in the glorious holy mountain; yet he shall come to his end, and none shall help him. (Daniel 11:45.)

Any attempt to understand the meaning of Daniel 11 necessitates a clear understanding of the phrase "glorious holy mountain." Any Israelite reading Daniel's words would know immediately what Daniel meant. To an Israelite, there was only one glorious holy mountain: Mount Zion.

> Great is the LORD, and greatly to be praised in the city of our God, in His holy mountain. Beautiful in elevation, the joy of the whole earth, is Mount Zion on the sides of the north, the city of the great King. (Psalm 48:1, 2, NKJV.)

Throughout the Old Testament, the term "Zion" was used as a reference to the nation of Israel. Originally, the name applied to the hill in the northernmost part of Jerusalem on which the temple was built. Eventually it came to symbolize the entire city of Jerusalem, and finally the whole nation of Israel. By the time of Daniel, the term "glorious holy mountain" or "Zion" was a clear reference to the people of the covenant, the nation of Israel.

According to Daniel 11:45, the focal point of the final attack by the king of the north is this glorious holy mountain. The Israel of God—His covenant people—are the ones who face the onslaught of the final attack of the enemy. Daniel 11:45 vividly portrays this for us. Many who preach about last-day events envision a gigantic battle in the Middle East between Arabs and Israelis, or a battle that in some way involves the nation of Israel now located in Palestine. If we were to take Daniel's statements literally, as many do, it would be relatively easy to arrive at that conclusion. However, if we are serious about discovering Bible truth, we will need to closely examine the Bible to find who it declares to be this final Israel.

If we apply the term "Israel" only to the people residing in Palestine, we have interpreted it in a strictly geographical sense. If we apply the term to all people of Jewish descent, then we have applied the term racially. However, if we apply the term spiritually, as the Bible does, we may well arrive at an entirely different conclusion than those who interpret it geographically or racially. In this chapter, we wish to clearly define the term "Israel" as set forth in the Bible.

The Origin of Israel

Nearly 2,000 years before the coming of Christ, God called a man by the name of Abram, living in Ur of the Chaldeans, to leave his roots and move to a new country. The wickedness of the surrounding culture was so severe that God deemed it necessary to remove this man and his family and create a new nation that would be faithful to God. In this way the knowledge of the true God would be preserved in the earth.

When Abram arrived in Canaan, God made two basic promises to him:

> And the LORD said unto Abram, after that Lot was separated from him, Lift up now thine eyes, and look from the place where thou art northward, and southward, and eastward, and westward: For all the land which thou seest, to thee will I give it, and to thy seed for ever. And I will make thy seed as the dust of the earth: so that if a man can number the dust of the earth, then shall thy seed also be numbered. (Genesis 13:14-16.)

Here were two promises: land and offspring. Both were promised to Abram as a part of the covenant God made with him. At first reading these promises seem to be normal promises of natural process. Simply put, God told Abram he would possess the land of Canaan to which he had been brought and that he would have many descendants.

Yet the New Testament amplifies our understanding of these basic covenantal promises and enables us to see them through God's eyes, rather than just Abram's. Here the promises are shown to have deep spiritual meaning.

> Now to Abraham and his seed were the promises made. He saith not, And to seeds, as of many; but as of one, And to thy seed, which is Christ. (Galatians 3:16.)

> For he looked for a city which hath foundations, whose builder and maker is God. (Hebrews 11:10.)

> But now they desire a better country, that is, an heavenly. (Hebrews 11:16.)

What a revelation! What appeared to be literal, physical promises at first glance are instead realized to be deeply spiritual promises when seen through God's eyes. Not only were offspring promised to Abraham, but *the* Offspring—Christ. What a glorious promise, that through Abram's progeny would come forth the Son of the Living God! It wasn't just the miserable Middle East that God promised ancient Abram, but the heavenly Canaan. Earthly Palestine was only a type of the heavenly land. The earthly was only a foretaste of the real promise. These seemingly literal promises were actually spiritual promises given to a person who had entered into a spiritual covenant with God. Anyone not in a spiritual relationship with God cannot inherit these promises solely by birth.

We see this premise demonstrated in those who followed Abram—later called Abraham. If the promises had been literal, they would have been given to all the physical descendants of Abraham, but instead we discover that they were given only to those who accepted the spiritual inheritance. Ishmael, for example, even though he was a son of Abraham, did not receive the promises. Only Isaac, the child of the promise, did.

Likewise, Isaac's two sons, Jacob and Esau, did

not both receive the promises. Esau, the man of the world, sells his birthright—the spiritual promises of the covenant. Jacob, the second-born son of Isaac, then becomes the inheritor of the spiritual promises. Thus, the promise of the Seed is through Jacob's descendants, not Esau's. As Jacob flees from home after receiving the blessing from Isaac, God again gives the land and seed promise to him (Genesis 28:13, 14).

After sojourning with Laban for over twenty years and marrying Rachel and Leah, Jacob returns to Palestine, the symbol of the heavenly Canaan. Even though Jacob had received the promise when he left Palestine, he still had failed to develop a strong and lasting relationship with God. Genesis 32 tells the story. As Jacob nears Canaan, he hears that Esau is approaching him with armed men. In desperation, he divides his company into two groups, hoping that at least part of his household will escape the inevitable destruction of the revengeful Esau. The next evening, having sent his family across the Jabbok river, Jacob is left alone. There he wrestles with the angel till the break of day. Notice the rest of the story:

> And when he saw that he prevailed not against him, he touched the hollow of his thigh; and the hollow of Jacob's thigh was out of joint, as he wrestled with him. And he said, Let me go, for the day breaketh. And he said, I will not let thee go, except thou bless me. And he said unto him, What is thy name? And he said, Jacob. And he said, Thy name shall be called no more Jacob, but Israel: for as a prince hast thou power with God and with men, and hast prevailed. (Genesis 32:25-28..

Here is the first mention of the name "Israel" in Scripture. It is applied to Jacob, whose name meant "supplanter," or "cheat." Having wrestled with the angel and prevailed with God, Jacob is now numbered with the overcomers. So he is given a name fit for a redeemed person. That name is "Israel," meaning "overcomer." Note the spiritual nature of the name, as well as the spiritual occasion on which it was given.

In examining the origin of Israel, we have discovered that the name originated in a spiritual context—given to a spiritual person, when he was converted to God. To belong to Israel was to receive the spiritual promises made to Abraham: the promise of Christ and the promise of the heavenly Canaan. Therefore, these promises cannot apply geographically or racially. They can only be applied spiritually. The origin of Israel necessitates a spiritual application of the terminology.

The Nation of Israel

The descendants of Israel (Jacob) eventually formed themselves into a nation that took on the covenant name of the father of the twelve tribes. Out of all the nations of earth, that nation was the only one that acknowledged the true God: At Mount Sinai, they entered into a covenant with God. As they became the converted people of God, they rightfully assumed the name of the covenant people: Israel. As long as they remained faithful to the covenant, they could rightfully be called Israelites. If they left the covenant people, they could no longer be called Israelites, even though they racially belonged to the descendants of Abraham.

Likewise, it was possible even for people not born

of Abraham's seed to become Israelites—and even progenitors of the Messiah. Two clear examples surface in the Old Testament in the lineage of Christ: Rahab, the harlot; and Ruth, the Moabitess. Ruth even became the grandmother of David, the mighty king of Israel. If the term "Israel" referred only to the literal descendants of Abraham, it would have been impossible for Gentiles to become Israelites, but these Old Testament examples clearly illustrate that they could. The term was not racial, but spiritual. Because Ruth and Rahab had accepted the God of Israel, they could become Israelites.

When the literal nation of Israel in the Old Testament sinned and left the Lord, God sent his prophets to inform them that they had become a harlot. Why? They were claiming to be Israelites, spiritual people, when they were not converted. A person cannot lay claim to the spiritual title, unless he or she is spiritual.

After the time of Solomon, the ten northern tribes separated from the two southern tribes. The northern kingdom took the name, "Israel" for its kingdom. The southern kingdom assumed the name "Judah." However, the northern tribes soon went into dreadful apostasy, from which they never recovered. Finally, they were carried away captive by the Assyrians. The southern kingdom likewise apostasized, but did keep their faith longer. Eventually, they too failed God and went into captivity in Babylon. Even though the northern kingdom claimed the title, they really were not Israel during this period of apostasy. For many years the southern kingdom actually had a greater right to the title, since they were faithful to God.

After the Babylonian captivity, remnants from all twelve tribes returned to Palestine. Although the majority were from the tribe of Judah, there were people from all tribes. This restored kingdom renewed the covenant with God and once again became Israel, the faithful people of the covenant. The term "Israel," in this stage of history, refers primarily to those people who returned in obedience to God from the Babylonian captivity. 1 Chronicles 9:3 mentions Judah, Benjamin, Ephraim, and Manasseh as being among the returned exiles. According to Ezra 6:14-17, they sacrificed twelve goats for the twelve tribes, and—according to Zechariah 8:3-5, 13—both the houses of Israel and Judah were among the returned exiles. It was these returned exiles, made up of all twelve tribes, who became the new Israel at this time. The spiritual term now applied to them.

Jesus and the Nation of Israel

For nearly 2,000 years, God had attempted to accomplish His work through the descendants of Abraham. Patiently God sought to use these people to bring the knowledge of God to the world. He placed them at the crossroads of civilization, but again and again they failed to share Him with the world that passed by. Yet, as perverted as their idea of God had become, they still were the only people on the face of the earth who acknowledged the true God. In desperation, God sent His Son to them, hoping that they would respond to Him, but instead they crucified Him. It was time for God's last appeal to the descendants of Abraham. Either they would respond and be drawn to Christ or God would have to call out a new Israel, consisting of a people who would be faithful to the spiritual promises given to Abraham. God was not dependent on an ethnic group to accomplish His purpose. Race did not matter with God. He had made all races. Faithfulness to the covenant was the only criterion.

As Jesus began His ministry, He quickly announced His mission to bring the final call of repentance to the literal nation of Israel.

> "Or those eighteen on whom the tower in Siloam fell and killed them, do you think that they were worse sinners than all other men who dwelt in Jerusalem?
>
> "I tell you, no; but unless you repent you will all likewise perish."
>
> He also spoke this parable: "A certain man had a fig tree planted in his vineyard, and he came seeking fruit on it and found none.
>
> "Then he said to the keeper of his vineyard, 'Look, for three years I have come seeking fruit on this fig tree and find none. Cut it down; why does it use up the ground?'
>
> "But he answered and said to him, 'Sir, let it alone this year also, until I dig around it and fertilize it.
>
> 'And if it bears fruit, well. But if not, after that you can cut it down'" (Luke 13:4-9, NKJV).

The Jews of Christ's day actually thought that salvation came through heredity. Jesus clearly informed them that salvation had nothing to do with genes, but everything to do with a relationship with God. How patient God is. After 2,000 years, He still hated to give up on Israel. For three years

Jesus had come seeking fruit of the fig tree, a symbol of Israel. He found none. Not much time was left for this people. If they did not respond, the privilege of being God's chosen people would actually be removed, as symbolized by the fig tree being cut down. Anxiously, God awaited their response.

> O Jerusalem, Jerusalem, which killest the prophets, and stonest them that are sent unto thee; how often would I have gathered thy children together, as a hen doth gather her brood under her wings, and ye would not! Behold, your house is left unto you desolate. (Luke 13:34, 35.)

Jesus did not want Israel to cease being His chosen nation. He wept over the coming loss of the people He had patiently cultivated for 2,000 years. Yet, unless they were gathered to Christ, they would be cut off. Their house, the temple, would be left devoid of the Spirit of God—desolate. How terrible the consequences of failing to accept the promised Seed—the ultimate fulfillment of the promise made to Abraham. After the time of Christ, only those who had accepted this ultimate fulfillment of the promise could still be Israelites. Jesus foretold Israel's coming doom in these sad words:

> And when he was come near, he beheld the city, and wept over it, Saying, If thou hadst known, even thou, at least in this thy day, the things which belong unto thy peace! but now they are hid from thine eyes. For the days shall come upon thee, that thine enemies shall cast a trench about thee, and compass thee round, and keep thee in on every side, And shall lay thee even with the ground, and thy children within thee; and they

shall not leave in thee one stone upon another; because thou knewest not the time of thy visitation. (Luke 19:41-44.)

Note the reason for this total rejection: "because thou knewest not the time of thy visitation." The issue was clear. Only those who accepted the Messiah and were gathered to Jesus could still be Israelites. Sadly, the rest would cease to be Israelites, even though they might still call themselves Israel. The term is spiritual and cannot be applied to an unspiritual people. In no uncertain words Christ announced the fall of Israel and the calling forth of a new Israel who accepted the provisions of the covenant; that is, the covenant's ultimate fulfillment—Jesus Christ:

> "Hear another parable: There was a certain landowner who planted a vineyard and set a hedge around it, dug a winepress in it and built a tower. And he leased it to vinedressers and went into a far country.

> "Now when vintage-time drew near, he sent his servants to the vinedressers, that they might receive its fruit.

> "And the vinedressers took his servants, beat one, killed one, and stoned another.

> "Again he sent other servants, more than the first, and they did likewise to them.

> "Then last of all he sent his son to them, saying, 'They will respect my son.'

> "But when the vinedressers saw the son, they said among themselves, 'This is the heir. Come, let us kill him and seize his inheritance.'

> "And they caught him, and cast him out of the vineyard, and killed him.

"Therefore, when the owner of the vineyard comes, what will he do to those vinedressers?"

'They said to Him, "He will destroy those wicked men miserably, and lease his vineyard to other vinedressers who will render to him the fruits in their seasons."'

Jesus said to them, "Did you never read in the Scriptures:

'The stone which the builders rejected
Has become the chief cornerstone.
This was the LORD's doing,
And it is marvelous in our eyes'?

"Therefore I say to you, the kingdom of God will be taken from you and given to a nation bearing the fruits of it." (Matthew 21:33-43, NKJV.)

The vineyard, a symbol of the privilege of being God's Israel, was to be removed from the original tenants, the descendants of Abraham, and given to a new people who would produce fruit. Here Jesus in unmistakable language announced the cessation of the literal nation of Israel as the chosen people, and the coming forth of a new people who would be faithful to the covenant promises. How would they be faithful? They would accept Jesus as the fulfillment of the covenant. The only way to become or remain an Israelite was to accept the covenant fulfillment: Jesus.

Daniel the prophet had warned Israel that seventy weeks were given to them to come into line (Daniel 9:24-27); otherwise they would be rejected. Daniel warned them that the Messiah would come in the last of the seventy weeks and attempt to confirm the covenant with them. That prophecy, beginning with the decree of Artaxerxes in 457

B.C., stretched to A.D. 27, when Jesus was baptized at the end of the sixty-nine weeks. (In Bible prophecy, a day stands for one year: Ezekiel 4:6.) For one more week—seven years—after the Messiah's arrival, the covenant would be confirmed with the Jews. As the prophecy predicted, in the middle of the seventieth week, Jesus brought an end to the sacrificial system by His death on Calvary's cross. Three and a half years later, at the end of the seventy weeks, the Jews sealed their rejection of the gospel by the stoning of Stephen. Their time had ended, just as Daniel had predicted. Now it was time for a new Israel to emerge. Of old Israel, only those who accepted the Messiah would be included. In addition, any person who received Jesus as Saviour and Lord would be numbered with the new Israel, regardless of national origin. Let us examine this new Israel that emerges between A.D. 31 and 34.

The New Israel

After the end of Daniel's seventy weeks in A.D. 34, a new Israel suddenly emerges. Even though the term "Israel" was considered an ethnic term in the first century, Paul reintroduced the Old Testament concept of Israel as a spiritual entity and not simply an inherent right of racial Israel.

> For he is not a Jew, which is one outwardly; neither is that circumcision, which is outward in the flesh: But he is a Jew, which is one inwardly; and circumcision is that of the heart, in the spirit, and not in the letter; whose praise is not of men, but of God. (Romans 2:28, 29.)

What makes a person a Jew or an Israelite, then, is not his physical genealogy but his spiritual relationship with Christ. Again, the term "Israel" has now become a spiritual term rather than an ethnic one. This is not a new thought, as we have seen, but a reaffirmation of biblical Judaism.

Paul continues this thought in Romans 9:6-8 (NIV):

> It is not as though God's word had failed. For not all who are descended from Israel are Israel. Nor because they are his descendants are they all Abraham's children. On the contrary, "It is through Isaac that your offspring will be reckoned. In other words, it is not the natural children who are God's children, but it is the children of the promise who are regarded as Abraham's offspring."

Only those who have accepted the promise—Christ—are true Israelites in the New Testament. To be born genetically of Abraham has no more merit with God than to be born of George Washington or Abraham Lincoln.

Genetic inheritance has no merit with God. All that matters is a person's relationship with Jesus Christ. To be an Israelite now, one must be born again spiritually.

While Israel is no longer ethnic in the New Testament, it is still possible for ethnic Jews to become a part of the true Israel, but only if they accept the Lord Jesus Christ. A person becomes an Israelite by faith, not by genealogy. Note as Paul continues in Romans 11:

> For I speak to you Gentiles; inasmuch as I am an apostle to the Gentiles, I magnify my ministry, if by any means I may provoke to jealousy those who are my flesh and save some of them. For if their being cast away is the reconciling of the

world, what will their acceptance be but life from
the dead? (Verses 13-15, NKJV.)

You will say then, "Branches were broken off that
I might be grafted in." Well said. Because of
unbelief they were broken off, and you stand by
faith. Do not be haughty, but fear. For if God did
not spare the natural branches, He may not spare
you either. (Verses 19-21, NKJV.)

And they also, if they do not continue in unbelief,
will be grafted in, for God is able to graft them in
again. (Verse 23, NKJV.)

This is the new Israel that Jesus Christ has
brought into being. It is made up of a people who
believe in Christ. Those who had preserved the
knowledge of the true God for nearly 2,000 years
were being cast away as the covenant people. Yet
many of them had become a part of this new Israel,
which was to become totally international. No racial or ethnic boundaries would be found in it.

For generations a gulf existed between Jews and
non-Jews. But by virtue of Calvary, that wall of
separation has been forever broken down. Christ
has called into being a new entity, a new Israel,
composed of Jews and Gentiles. That new Israel is
the Christian church.

For he is our peace, who hath made both one, and
hath broken down the middle wall of partition
between us. (Ephesians 2:14.)

And that he might reconcile both unto God in
one body by the cross, having slain the enmity
thereby. (Ephesians 2:16.)

Now therefore ye are no more strangers and
foreigners, but fellowcitizens with the saints, and
of the household of God; And are built upon the

foundation of the apostles and prophets, Jesus Christ himself being the chief corner stone; In whom all the building fitly framed together groweth unto an holy temple in the Lord. (Ephesians 2:19-21.)

This new body—this new Israel—has no barriers to separate people by race or national origin. The new Israel is international in character. It is based on spiritual issues, not on ethnic issues. However, Paul does not end here; he goes one step further in Galatians 3:28, 29:

There is neither Jew nor Greek, there is neither bond nor free, there is neither male nor female; for ye are all one in Christ Jesus. And if ye be Christ's then are ye Abraham's seed, and heirs according to the promise.

Amazing! No salvation by race with Jesus! All people are one in Christ Jesus our Lord. Paul's startling conclusion is that this new entity created by Christ, the Christian church—into which people of all nations have been born by accepting Christ—is the new Israel.

All who belong to Christ are now Abraham's seed—Jews. They are the inheritors of the promise made to Abraham. They are the heirs of the promise. As a result, Christians become the rightful heirs to all Old Testament promises made to Israel. Hence, in New Testament time, according to the apostle Paul, we are no longer to look for a fulfillment of the Old Testament promises given to ancient Israel in the literal nation. Spiritual Israel, the Christian church, now inherits all of these promises.

Any prophecy referring to Israel that is fulfilled

after the cross will be fulfilled, not in the ethnic nation of Israel, but in the new Israel called forth by Christ—the Christian Church. This startling, overwhelming conclusion of Paul's must have shaken ancient Judaism to its very core. They had made so much of their ancestry, but now Paul declares that the rightful heirs to that status are only those who are gathered to Christ.

Applying the Prophetic Principle

The New Testament has given us a very basic principle of interpretation. Both Jesus and Paul have affirmed the existence of a new Israel after the cross that inherits all of the Old Testament prophecies of Israel. What failed to be fulfilled in ancient Israel will be fulfilled in the new Israel of the New Testament. Thus all Old Testament prophecies of Israel are to be reinterpreted through the eyes of the New Testament if fulfillment is found after A.D. 34.

Notice how this principle works. In Joel 2:32 a prophecy reaching to the end times is given. This prophecy focuses specifically on a geographical location: Mount Zion and Jerusalem.

> And it shall come to pass, that whosoever shall call on the name of the LORD shall be delivered: for in mount Zion and in Jerusalem shall be deliverance, as the LORD hath said, and in the remnant whom the LORD shall call.

If we took this passage literally, without its New Testament reinterpretation, it would be easy to conclude that salvation in the end time will be found only by those who travel to Jerusalem and stand on Mount Zion. However, if we accept the New Testament's clear teaching that Israel after the cross refers to the church, then we can conclude that deliverance in the last days will be in the Christian Church. There is no need to buy plane tickets. In the New Testament, Jerusalem refers to the Christian Church, not to a geographical city (Hebrews 12:22, 23). Both Jerusalem and Mount Zion refer to the church. To deny this is to deny the basic New Testament concept of the church.

Likewise, in Luke 21:24 Jesus predicted that Jerusalem would be trampled by the Gentiles until the times of the Gentiles would be fulfilled. If we read this text without the New Testament understanding of Israel, it would be possible to conclude that when Jerusalem is given back to the ethnic Jews, the prophecy would be fulfilled. Some have made such an interpretation, and have concluded that the times of the Gentiles ended in either 1948 with the establishment of the Israeli state or in 1967 when Israel repossessed ancient Jerusalem. In either case, it would mean that the time of the Gentiles was ended—a strange interpretation indeed for Christians today.

On the other hand, if Jerusalem refers to the church, as Hebrews 12:22, 23 indicates, then it is the church that is trodden under foot or dominated by an apostate power for a specified period of time. Revelation 11:2, 3 helps us better understand Jesus' prophecy:

> But the court which is without the temple leave out, and measure it not; for it is given unto the Gentiles: and the holy city shall they tread under foot forty and two months. And I will give power unto my two witnesses, and they shall prophecy a thousand two hundred and threescore days, clothed in sackcloth.

John the Revelator enables us to discover that the times of the Gentiles are forty-two months, or 1260 years. Here is a clear biblical reference to the 1260 years during which the apostate power dominated the church (see chapter 2). These two passages make complete sense when we attempt to apply them to the church, but are confusing interpretations when we fail to apply the New Testament interpretation of Israel.

Will all prophecies of the Old Testament referring to Israel be fulfilled? No. There are prophecies that refer to a glorious future for the nation of Israel and there are prophecies that refer to a scattering among the nations. Obviously, both cannot be fulfilled. God has predicted in the Old Testament what would happen if Israel were faithful and also what would happen if it were unfaithful. Since ethnic Israel was unfaithful, those promises were fulfilled that predicted her scattering. The promises of the glorious future either never will be fulfilled or will be reinterpreted in the New Testament to refer to the church. Here we must exercise caution. It is not our responsibility to reinterpret— only inspired writers can do that for us. We must be careful not to try to find a literal fulfillment for every prophecy concerning Israel. Instead, let us examine the New Testament to discover if a reinterpretation has indeed been made.

This type of prophecy, found in the Old Testament, is called conditional prophecy. In fact, prophecies involving human choice are always conditional. Jeremiah, God's prophet of doom for Israel before the Babylonian captivity, made this point very clear:

> At what instant I shall speak concerning a nation,
> and concerning a kingdom, to pluck up, and to
> pull down, and to destroy it; If that nation,
> against whom I have pronounced, turn from
> their evil, I will repent of the evil that I thought
> to do unto them. And at what instant I shall speak
> concerning a nation, and concerning a kingdom,
> to build and to plant it; If it do evil in my sight,
> that it obey not my voice, then I will repent of the
> good, wherewith I said I would benefit them.
> (Jeremiah 18:7-10.)

God is not required in every prophecy to state
that it is conditional upon people's response. He
has given us a categorical statement in this passage. We should not, then, expect to see a literal
fulfillment of many of these Old Testament promises to ancient Israel. The only fulfillment we can
look for is in the Christian Church, as the New
Testament reinterprets it for us.

Some have felt that Jeremiah's prophecies in Jeremiah 30:3, 11 and 31:8, 9 that predict a return of
Israel from the places they were scattered refers to
the return of the Jews to Palestine in 1948. However, Israel in 1948 is no longer ethnic—it is spiritual, the Christian church. Therefore any return
must be reinterpreted through the New Testament.

Yet, when one examines these prophecies given
by Jeremiah just before the Babylonian captivity, it
becomes very clear that Jeremiah is referring to the
seventy-year captivity in Babylon and gives the
Jews the prediction that they would return to Palestine after the captivity. That was fulfilled. The
Babylonian captivity is the focus and the context
of Jeremiah's prediction. To refer the prophecy to

the last day is to deny the historical context of the prophet's own writing.

Will there be an eschatological gathering? Yes, but not of literal Jews. The New Testament reinterprets the gathering predictions in light of the new Israel called forth by Christ.

> And this spake he not of himself: but being high priest that year, he prophesied that Jesus should die for that nation; And not for that nation only, but that also he should gather together in one the children of God that were scattered abroad. (John 11:51, 52.)

Any gathering is a Christian gathering. God gives no special favors to any people because of their genealogy. The only ones who fulfill the gathering promises for Israel in the Old Testament are Christians who are gathered into one new body by Christ. This is how the New Testament reinterprets the gathering promises.

The Glorious Holy Mountain

Daniel 11:45 predicts that at the time of the end, the final king of the north will attempt to place his tabernacle in the glorious holy mountain. We have discovered this mountain to be Mount Zion. Since this is a reference to the last days, Mount Zion can only refer to the Christian church and not to a specific nation, people, or place in the Middle East. Daniel 11:45 is describing Satan's final attack against the church of the Living God.

According to the New Testament, the focus of last-day events is not the nation of Israel, but the church of Jesus Christ. This is where the action is in the last days. By trying to interpret the holy mountain as a literal place in the Middle East,

Satan today is attempting to cause people to focus on the wrong events. Last-day events do not center around oil fields and military conquests in the Middle East. Last-day events focus on God's people, whom Satan wishes to destroy. This thought will be further explored in a future chapter, after we have put all the pieces together. First of all, we need to identify the final king of the north in Daniel 11. That is the subject of the next chapter.

5

The King of the North

The most dominant symbol throughout Daniel 11 is that of the "king of the north." Interestingly, we have discovered that this symbol changes meanings as the chapter progresses. It begins as one of the divisions of the Grecian empire, then is used to symbolize the pagan Roman Empire, and emerges finally as the great apostasy that controlled the church of the Dark Ages.

In verses 40-45, it seems to gain renewed strength as it attacks the beautiful holy mountain.

It would appear that Daniel is seeking to convey a deeper truth through the use of this symbol than we might glean from just a quick examination of the chapter. Who really is this king of the north?

The Original King of the North

While the king of the north in Daniel 11 primarily refers to powers that were against the covenant people, this symbolism is used elsewhere in Scripture to indicate that God Himself is the original King of the North. In fact, God is the only true King of the North. Any others who claim this title are usurpers.

Throughout the Old Testament, north was the point of the compass assigned to God. It was the place from which God ruled. In Leviticus 1:11 the sacrifice was said to be killed on the north side of the altar and that the north side was before the Lord. Perhaps the most significant text on this point is Psalm 48:1, 2:

> Great is the Lord, and greatly to be praised in the city of our God, in the mountain of his holiness. Beautiful for situation, the joy of the whole earth, is mount Zion, on the side of the north, the city of the great King.

Mount Zion, the city of God, the place from which God ruled ancient Israel, was said to be on the side of the north. Ancient Jerusalem contained two hills; the northernmost one was Zion. It is the place where Solomon later built the temple. In the temple was the Shekinah glory, the literal presence of God on earth. Ezekiel the prophet was taken to the north gate of the temple, where the rebellious Israelites had erected an image of jealousy. There Ezekiel saw the glory of God at the north gate (Ezekiel 8:3, 4). Thus, it would be logical for the ancient Jews to look to the north as the place where God's presence was—the place from which He ruled.

Perhaps Daniel was familiar with Isaiah's statement that God would raise up a deliverer for His
people from the Babylonian captivity. That deliverer, Isaiah declared, would come from the north
and from the east (Isaiah 41:25). While this primarily referred to Cyrus, who rescued God's people
from Babylon, yet other Scriptures seem to employ
it as a type of the final deliverance of God's people.
There may be a reference to this in Daniel 11:44:
"Tidings out of the east and out of the north shall
trouble him." The Old Testament seems to indicate
north as the direction from which God will deliver
His people.

Satan the Usurper As King of the North

In Daniel 11, the great controversy between
Christ and Satan is being played out in a pictorial
drama. Satan has attempted to usurp God's throne.
This struggle has been going on since sin first
entered the universe. Lucifer, the highest of God's
created beings, rebelled against God. Pride arose
in his heart, and he determined that he could rule
better than God could. Lucifer wanted to take over
God's position as king of the North. So he accused
God of being unjust and claimed that nobody
could keep God's law. He insisted that God was
asking an impossibility of His created beings.

As a result of Lucifer's rebellion, one third of the
heavenly host sided with him in the conflict, and
they were all cast out of heaven. The warfare that
began in heaven now continued on the earth. Soon
Lucifer, who became Satan, seduced Adam and
Eve to sin. Satan then claimed to be the prince of
this world—the king of the north, ruler of planet
earth. After all, Adam and Eve had agreed to his

rulership. That which God had ruled so perfectly, Satan had now stolen, and he laid claim to the title "king of the north."

God describes this battle for the control of the north in Isaiah 14:13:

> For thou hast said in thine heart, I will ascend into heaven, I will exalt my throne above the stars of God: I will sit also upon the mount of the congregation, in the sides of the north.

So Lucifer, or Satan, originally desired to sit upon, or control, Mount Zion from the sides of the north. Scripture declares that God is the original ruler of Planet Earth, but Satan has usurped God's authority and now claims that he is the rightful king of the north. The battle for the control of this earth is the battle of the great controversy. This is the primary issue in last-day events.

Today Mount Zion refers to the church of Jesus Christ (Hebrews 12:22, 23—and see the previous chapter). Satan is portrayed in both the Old and New Testaments as constantly attempting to control and dominate God's Church. He claims to be the only king of the north, and the battle for the control of Mount Zion is his final attempt to dominate the church of the last days. Daniel 11:40-45 portrays Satan as the final king of the north as he attempts to capture Mount Zion—God's last-day church.

This same battle is pictured in Revelation 12:17, where Satan wages war against the woman and her remnant who keep the commandments of God and have the testimony of Jesus Christ. The result of this battle is clearly portrayed in Daniel 12:1, when Michael, the true king of the North, stands up and delivers God's people.

In Daniel 11, the prophet has portrayed for us through one symbol—the king of the north—the one power behind all earthly powers, who has attempted to destroy the covenant people of God. That power is Satan. This is why only one symbol is used for Greece, Rome, and the apostasy of the Dark Ages.

In Old Testament times the whole world had given Satan allegiance except for Palestine. That's why he waged war there, and that's why warfare in Palestine figured so prominently in biblical history. Only those nations that affected the covenant people are portrayed in Scripture, and only those battles involving the covenant people are recorded. Why? Because Scripture is only interested in portraying the great controversy theme for us. Only nations in conflict with Israel and Israel's God are brought to view in the Scriptures and its prophecies.

Likewise, in the last days the whole world will give allegiance to Satan, except for the remnant of Revelation 12:17. If Satan could conquer them, his power would be complete. All would then yield to his control. That's why the focal point of last-day events becomes the final Israel—the remnant of Revelation 12:17. Against this people all the fiery darts of the wicked one will be hurled. Last-day events will center on this remnant, which is symbolized by the beautiful holy mountain. Final events will not focus on the Middle East but on God's people, whom Satan is seeking to eliminate from the face of the earth.

The King of the North in History

In Old Testament times the enemies of God's

people are always presented as coming from the north:

> Set up the standard toward Zion: retire, stay not: for I will bring evil from the north, and a great destruction. (Jeremiah: 4:6.)

> Therefore thus saith the Lord of hosts; Because ye have not heard my words, Behold, I will send and take all the families of the north, saith the LORD, and Nebuchadnezzar the king of Babylon, my servant, and will bring them against this land, and against the inhabitants thereof, and against all these nations round about, and will utterly destroy them, and make them an astonishment, and an hissing, and perpetual desolations. (Jeremiah 25:8, 9.)

> For this is the day of the Lord GOD of hosts, a day of vengeance, that he may avenge him of his adversaries: and the sword shall devour, and it shall be satiate and made drunk with their blood: for the Lord GOD of hosts hath a sacrifice in the north country by the river Euphrates. (Jeremiah 46:10.)

So God allowed Satan, the usurped king of the north, to work through such nations as Babylon to bring judgment on His rebellious people. The point is that Satan can only do something to Zion if God permits. Satan tried continually to destroy Zion, but was checked by God. Only when the people of God had filled their cup of iniquity did God withdraw His protection from Jerusalem, which permitted Satan to move the armies of Babylon against it. Nevertheless, God was still in full control.

> In the annals of human history, the growth of nations, the rise and fall of empires, appear as dependent on the will and prowess of man. The

shaping of events seems, to a great degree, to be determined by his power, ambition, or caprice. But in the word of God the curtain is drawn aside, and we behold behind, above, and through all the play and counterplay of human interests and power and passions, the agencies of the all merciful One, silently, patiently working out the counsels of His own will.—E. G. White, *Education*, p. 178.

As the wheellike complications were under guidance of the hand beneath the wings of the cherubim, so the complicated play of human events is under divine control. Amidst the strife and tumult of nations, He that sitteth above the cherubim still guides the affairs of earth.—*Ibid.*

While ancient Babylon was the king of the north to ancient Israel, even so spiritual Babylon becomes the king of the north in New Testament times, as portrayed in the Book of Revelation.

So he carried me away in the Spirit into the wilderness. And I saw a woman sitting on a scarlet beast which was full of names of blasphemy, having seven heads and ten horns.

The woman was arrayed in purple and scarlet, and adorned with gold and precious stones and pearls, having in her hand a golden cup full of abominations and the filthiness of her fornication.

And on her forehead a name was written: MYSTERY, BABYLON THE GREAT, THE MOTHER OF HARLOTS AND OF THE ABOMINATIONS OF THE EARTH.

I saw the woman, drunk with the blood of the saints and with the blood of the martyrs of Jesus . . .

Here is the mind with wisdom: The seven heads
are seven mountains on which the woman sits.
(Revelation 17:3-6, 9, NKJV.)

Revelation 17 is a clear picture of the sad con-
dition of the church in the Dark Ages (see chapter
2). Just as ancient Babylon was the enemy of
God's people and sought to destroy them, so
spiritual Babylon became the great enemy of
God's people during the Dark Ages. Through
persecution of saints and the corruption of doctrine, she attempted to dominate the world. Just
as ancient Babylon was called the king of the
north when Satan worked through her to destroy
God's people, so spiritual Babylon became the
king of the north when she sought to destroy
God's people in the Dark Ages. Any power that
seeks to dominate God's saints is the king of the
north.

Revelation 13:11-17 pictures a revival of apostate
religion, united with the state and reactivated for
the purpose of destroying God's people in the final
conflict. A death decree is even passed against
those who are faithful to God, and no one is allowed to buy or sell unless they have the mark of
this apostate religious power of the last days.
Nearly the whole Christian world followed this
apostasy in the Middle Ages; even so in the last
days, all except the remnant of Revelation 12:17
will follow this revived system. This final power
will involve an apostate Romanism and an apostate Protestantism, combined with spiritualistic in-
fluences to wage the final war against God's
people.

In Daniel 11:1-39 the prophet has traced the king

of the north through Greece, pagan Rome, and the apostate church of the Dark Ages. Thus when we arrive at the time of the end in verse 40, the king of the north is still the church of the Dark Ages. Daniel 11:40-45 describes the king of the north that reappears at the end time.

This is the same power described in Revelation 13:11-17: the three-fold union of apostate Romanism and apostate Protestantism, united by spiritualism. When this final king of the north emerges, he will wage earth's final battle against God's Israel. This battle is described in Daniel 11:45; Revelation 12:17, and Revelation 13:11-17. It is also described as the battle of Armageddon in Revelation 16. So it is that Satan the usurper unites the whole world in one final desperate attempt to gain control.

The good news is that God intervenes in this battle and delivers His people. All may appear to be lost, but it is not. All of the passages that describe this final battle point to the ultimate vindication of God and His people. The important thing to remember as we near the closing scenes of earth's history is to be on God's side in this final battle. If ever there was a time when we need to make certain that we have a deep personal relationship with Jesus Christ, it is now.

Satan's masterpiece of deception is about to be unveiled. It will engulf many sincere Christians, just as the deceptions of the Dark Ages destroyed the faith of many. We must be on our guard. Religious apostasy is in the very air we breathe in these last days. The only safety is in a relationship with God and in constant study of His Word. To be secure, we must test everything by the Bible and the Bible only.

6

The King of the South

God is the true king of the north, but Satan has worked through Persia, Greece, Rome, and the church of the Dark Ages in an attempt to usurp the title for himself and to destroy the covenant people of God.

In the last days, Satan will wage warfare against the remnant of Revelation 12:17. Through the threefold union of the papacy, apostate Protestantism, and spiritualism, Satan will seek to engage the world in the battle that will close the great controversy.

This will be Satan's final attempt to plant his tabernacle in the glorious holy mountain. Yet, before Satan can accomplish this, he must eliminate the king of the south.

Identity of the King of the South

In Daniel 11 the king of the south appears initially as one of the divisions of the Grecian empire. In particular, this title referred to the Egyptian division under the Ptolemies. This symbolism is maintained from verses 5 to 30. Especially from verse 25 onward, the king of the south seems to be losing power to the king of the north, until finally the king of the north becomes predominant.

For all practical purposes, Egypt as a major power ended in 31 B.C. in the battle of Accius, when Octavius defeated the forces of Marcus Antonius and Cleopatra. Egypt was then transformed into a Roman province. It has never regained its powerful, prestigious position. Today, Egypt is just one of the many countries of the Arab world.

Interestingly, Egypt—or the king of the south—totally disappears from the Daniel 11 narrative through verses 31-39. This is the time when the king of the north is dominant. During this period the king of the north symbolized the church of the Dark Ages. During the 1260 years of papal supremacy, we discover no reference in Daniel 11 to the king of the south. As long as religion controlled the western world politically, the king of the south was dead.

Suddenly, in Daniel 11:40, the king of the south reappears, entering the arena with great fury. Daniel 11:40 brings us to the biblical time of the end, when the reign of the little horn ends and Christ comes the second time. It begins in A.D. 1798 at the conclusion of the 1260-year prophecy. When the church of the Dark Ages loses her political arm, we see a reemergence of the king of the south. Note again Daniel 11:40:

> And at the time of the end shall the king of the south push at him: and the king of the north shall come against him like a whirlwind, with chariots, and with horsemen, and with many ships; and he shall enter into the countries, and shall overflow and pass over.

Who is this king of the south that suddenly reappears at the time of the end, around 1798? What power attacks the king of the north, the medieval papacy, at this time? It certainly was not Egypt, which was far from being a major power at this time. Since the imagery of the king of the north has changed meaning as history progressed, it would be logical also to assume that the symbol of the king of the south has changed meaning as well. Therefore, to discover the identity of the king of the south at the time of the end, we would need to ask, What kind of power was ancient Egypt? How did Egypt relate to the covenant people? Do we find a connecting link spiritually in Scripture to the power that brings an end to the papal supremacy of the Middle Ages and Egypt? We will discover the answer in Revelation 11:8 (NIV):

> Their bodies will lie in the street of the great city, which is figuratively called Sodom and Egypt, where also their Lord was crucified.

Here is a power linked spiritually to Egypt, the king of the south. It is a power, we discover, that alludes to the French Revolution at the end of the eighteenth century.

The Link of Egypt and France

Egypt's most notable confrontation with the God of Israel took place nearly 1,500 years before

Christ, when Moses stood before ancient Pharaoh and demanded that Egypt let God's people go from Egyptian captivity. The reply of Pharaoh to Moses' request is indicative of the kind of power Egypt was, in relationship to the God of the covenant. Note Exodus 5:1, 2:

> And afterward Moses and Aaron went in, and told Pharaoh, Thus saith the LORD God of Israel, Let my people go, that they may hold a feast unto me in the wilderness. And Pharaoh said, Who is the LORD, that I should obey his voice to let Israel go? I know not the LORD, neither will I let Israel go.

This is atheism. Pharaoh not only refused to obey God, but he also failed to recognize the existence of the God of Israel. Throughout biblical history, Egypt became a symbol of a defiant atheism that denies or ignores the existence of the one true God. Even as late as the Babylonian captivity, the prophet Ezekiel equated Egypt with atheism because of her claim to have created the Nile:

> Speak, and say, Thus saith the Lord GOD; Behold, I am against thee, Pharaoh king of Egypt, the great dragon that lieth in the midst of his rivers, which hath said, My river is mine own, and I have made it for myself. (Ezekiel 29:3.)

> And the land of Egypt shall be desolate and waste; and they shall know that I am the LORD: because he hath said, The river is mine, and I have made it. (Ezekiel 29:9.)

With biblical analogy linking Egypt to atheistic philosophy, it would be logical to discover that the nation represented by the king of the south in the time of the end when it attacks the medieval papacy would also be characterized by its atheistic philosophy. One biblical commentator saw this connection very clearly:

> Of all nations presented in Bible history, Egypt most boldly denied the existence of the living God and resisted His commands. No monarch ever ventured upon more open and highhanded rebellion against the authority of Heaven than did the king of Egypt. When the message was brought him by Moses, in the name of the Lord, Pharaoh proudly answered: "Who is Jehovah, that I should hearken unto His voice to let Israel go? I know not Jehovah, and moreover I will not let Israel go." Exodus 5:2, A.R.V. This is atheism, and the nation represented by Egypt would give voice to a similar denial of the claims of the living God and would manifest a like spirit of unbelief and defiance.—E. G. White, *The Great Controversy*, p. 269.

If we are reasoning correctly, Daniel 11 is predicting that around the time of the end, 1798, an atheistic power similar to Egypt would arise as the renewed king of the south. Its first business would be to attack the king of the north, the papacy, and to inflict on him a deadly wound. Then, having defeated the king of the north, atheism would become the dominant philosophy operating in the world. Did such a power arise around 1798 and do the very things predicted in Daniel 11? Amazingly, it did!

Revelation 11 and the King of the South

Revelation 11 opens around the time of the conclusion of the 1260-year prophecy (Revelation 11:1-3). For 1260 years God's two witnesses, clothed in sackcloth, preached to the people. The Bible could not be publicly proclaimed because of the political power of the medieval papacy. Who are these two witnesses who maintained a witness to God's truth for 1260 years? John the Revelator identifies them as follows:

> These are the two olive trees, and the two candlesticks standing before the God of the earth. (Revelation 11:4.)

Zechariah 4:1-6 identifies the two olive trees as the word of the Lord spoken to Zerubbabel by the Holy Spirit. Psalm 119:105 also identifies God's Word with lamps. It would appear that the Scriptures use the symbol of the two witnesses, represented by the olive trees and the lampstands, to be symbols of the Word of God. To us today, they would symbolize the Word of God as given in the Bible, which bears witness to the truth of God in both the Old and the New Testaments.

After these two sackcloth-garbed witnesses have given their testimony for 1260 years, the beast arises out of the bottomless pit, attacks them, and kills them (Revelation 11:7). The Scriptures during the Dark Ages silently bore witness to the truth of God. The Bible was kept from the people but was miraculously preserved. The power which arises around 1798 attacks the Bible—rather than keeping it from the people as the medieval papacy had done—and actually seeks its elimination from the earth.

The power which arises around 1798, at the very time the king of the south is reactivated in Daniel 11:40, is also a power that is linked to Egypt in Revelation 11:8. This is an unmistakable reference to the French Revolution at the end of the eighteenth century. During this time, France totally rebelled against medieval Catholicism, against the papacy, and against all religion, and tried to institute atheism. This revolution began in 1789 and continued to 1801. It was one of the most trying times in the history of France and Europe. Its implications continue well beyond the scope of the actual Revolution, as we shall shortly see.

Atheism reached its height in France from November 26, 1793, when the decree abolishing religion was issued in Paris, to June 17, 1797, when the restriction against religion was removed. Amazingly, this terrible period lasted for exactly three and a half years, just as predicted in Revelation 11:9. (Three and a half days equals three and a half years, using the day-for-a-year principle. Ezekiel 4:6.)

During this time the Bible was banned, a ten-day week was instituted to destroy God's seven-day week, and the goddess of reason (a naked woman) was enthroned as the god of France:

> The changing of the calendar was the prelude to the abolition of Christianity. The commune proposed this impious act to the Convention, and the Convention, becoming a party to it, decreed the replacement of the Catholic cult by the cult of Reason. This deplorable scandal, addresses in honor of atheism, and indecent abjurations, for the most part forced, figured in the official report sent to the authorities and to the armies. The poet Chenier composed a hymn in which, as a faithful disciple of Voltaire, he made open warfare upon the religion of Jesus Christ."—E. L. Higgins, *The French Revolution as Told by Contemporaries* (Boston: Houghton, 1938), p. 329.

I failed to witness the more than scandalous scenes in the Church of Notre Dame, where an actress of the opera was worshipped as a divinity, and I must say that most of the members of the Convention refused to be present at this. A large number even stopped attending the Assembly after the Bishop of Paris was brought to the bar to declare that he was an impostor, that he had never been anything else, and that the people were rejecting Christianity. His example was followed by priests and Protestant ministers in the Convention, who mounted the tribune to abdicate their religious offices. Some of the deputies became so disgusted and indignant that they ceased to appear in this dishonored Convention. The Montagnards perceived their absence, however, and forced them to return. They were compelled to listen daily to the most scandalous addresses, and to the recital of profanations committed by the imitators of the commune in the departments."— *Ibid*, p. 329, 330.

Such were the excesses of atheism impressed on the people. Such was also the state's response to the tragic excesses of religion during the Dark Ages. France, in rejecting Romanism, rejected all religion. In its stead, the nation's leaders inaugurated their Age of Reason. Their attacks were directed not only at the clergy, but at Christ Himself. The licentiousness and immorality that followed were disgusting. No wonder the Book of Revelation equates this Revolution to Egypt, Sodom, and Jerusalem: Egypt for its atheism, Sodom for its immorality, and Jerusalem for its attacks against Christ (Revelation 11:8). This terrible reign of terror lasted three and a half years. Finally, order was restored and religion once again was tolerated in

France. Since then, we have seen the Bible arise from the ashes of destruction inflicted by the Revolution to new heights of world-wide distribution (Revelation 11:11, 12).

Like Egypt of old, France during the Revolution defied the God of heaven and tried to institute atheism. While radical atheism died, the ideas of the French Revolution did not die. Even today, this period is recognized as the beginning of the modern atheistic movement. Much of secular thought can be traced to ideas that sprang from this Revolution.

France Inflicts the Deadly Wound

Revelation 11 has clearly linked the atheistic French Revolution to the major force that arose at the end of the 1260 years of papal supremacy. Daniel 11 predicted that the king of the south would become revitalized at the time of the end and would launch a vicious attack against the king of the north (Daniel 11:40). This attack would occur, according to Daniel 11:40, at the time of the end, which we have understood to begin in 1798, at the end of the 1260-year prophecy.

In the aftermath of the French Revolution, attacks by the French against the papacy increased. Finally, Berthier, the French general under Napoleon, actually invaded the Vatican, took the Pope prisoner, and ended the temporal sovereignty of the Pope. No longer would the papacy be a secular power. It was reduced to being only a religious power. The result of the French Revolution was the smashing of the medieval papacy, accurately foretold in Daniel 11:40.

When, in 1797, Pope Pius VI fell grievously ill,

Napoleon gave orders that in the event of his death no successor should be elected to his office, and that the papacy should be discontinued.

But the Pope recovered; the peace was soon broken; Berthier entered Rome on 10th February 1798, and proclaimed a Republic. The aged Pontiff refused to violate his oath by recognizing it, and was hurried from prison to prison into France. Broken with fatigue and sorrows, he died . . . [in] August 1799, in the French fortress of Valence, aged 82 years. No wonder that half of Europe thought Napoleon's veto would be obeyed, and that with the Pope the Papacy was dead.—Joseph Rickaby, "The Modern Papacy," in *Lectures on the History of Religions*, Vol. 3 [lecture 24, p. 1] (London: Catholic Truth Society, 1910).

Suddenly, the power of the medieval papacy—the king of the north at that time—was broken. His power seemed at its end. But remember, Daniel 11 foretells a revival of the king of the north after this. Yet, as the new century was about to dawn, it appeared as if the king of the south had triumphed and that the king of the north lay dead.

The Expansion of the French Revolution

While the excesses of the French Revolution soon subsided and order was restored, the ideas generated during this convulsive time in history did not die. Since 1798 there has been a world-wide dissemination of the ideas first fostered in the French Revolution. In a certain sense, the French Revolution marked a turning point in history. No longer would religion be the controlling element in society. Reason had seemingly won.

Shortly after the Revolution, atheistic leaders began to arise whose thought patterns expanded well beyond the boundaries of France. Yet most of these leaders looked back to the French Revolution as the source for their new ideas. In the area of religion, men such as George Hegel arose. Hegel became the father of modern atheism in philosophy and theology. Through him, higher criticism of the Bible entered the church. For the first time, people began to criticize the Bible as a divine Book. No longer was it to be blindly accepted.

In the area of science, men like Charles Darwin arose. Until this time, a literal creation had been accepted as truth by both science and religion. Now Darwin proposed that human life did not originate a few thousand years ago but evolved over countless millions of years. His conclusions sent shock waves across the religious world. Eventually, his ideas gained nearly universal acceptance in the scientific world. It now appeared that a new order was governing world affairs. No longer would God be viewed as the major force in society. Now secularism would dominate, and religion would be totally divorced from the governing part of society. Evolutionary philosophy, with its "survival of the fittest" motif, would be the guiding principle in the lives of people and in the governing of the world.

Around the same time that Darwin proclaimed his evolutionary theory, another leader arose: Karl Marx. Marx readily accepted Darwin's *Origin of Species* and united his own philosophies with it. What emerged eventually became known as godless communism. Soon Marx's ideas spread and found a stronghold in Russia with the communist revolution. Eventually the entire eastern bloc of Europe, China, and a good share of the developing nations of earth accepted the communist belief system.

In Western society there was a general rejection of the communist ideal, but not of its secularistic and atheistic tendencies. While atheism flourished in Russia under the iron rule of communism, Western nations abandoned their divine philosophies of government and education, and imbibed instead a secular humanism that has dominated most of Western society for the past several decades.

During most of the twentieth century it has appeared that the king of the south, represented by godless communism and secular humanism in the West, has become the dominant philosophy of the world. Religion has grown weaker and weaker. While Christianity as a percentage of the world's population declined from 34.4 percent of the world population in 1900 to 32.8 percent by 1980, atheism increased from 2 percent in 1900 to 20.8 percent by 1980. As we near the end of the twentieth century, it appears that the ideas of the French Revolution have triumphed in the world. The king of the south has indeed attacked the king of the north. Seemingly, he has even won the battle. But Daniel 11 predicts a revival of the king of the north that would attack the king of the south. We will examine the exciting fulfillment of the revival of the king of the north in the next chapter.

Thus, since 1798 and the infliction of the deadly wound, and in the aftermath of the French Revolution, we have seen the rise of the king of the south as a major power once again. We have also seen the world-wide penetration of the ideas of the French Revolution, until it appears that atheism and secular philosophy are in control of most of the world, not only in communist lands, but in Western thought as well. But a change is due. As we prepare for the climax of the ages, we will watch the rebirth of religious intolerance once again, as the king of the north reappears and attacks the king of the south. That battle is now going on!

7

The King of the North Reemerges

Rebellion arose before the creation of this world, in the very gates of Paradise itself. Lucifer, the highest of God's created beings, decided he could rule better than God could. He contended that God's law was unfair, unjust, and could not be kept. If the angels of heaven would only follow him, he boasted, he would lead them to a better way of life. Lucifer's suggestions were so devious that one third of the heavenly angels sided with him and rebelled against God. God, rather than ordering the destruction of these errant angels, allowed them to continue their insubordination. That made it possible for the rest of the universe to see the natural outworking of evil. If God had destroyed them immediately, the whole universe would have served God out of fear rather than love. The only obedience acceptable to God was that which sprang from love.

The rebellion begun in heaven continued on earth, when Lucifer, now called Satan, induced Adam and Eve to sin. This earth became the theater of the universe, where the drama of the great controversy was to be played out. For 6,000 years this controversy has continued. The universe can now see what Satan's reign is like. After all this time, he still lives in rebellion against God. The final events of the great controversy are about to unfold as Satan launches his final attack against the few on earth who acknowledge the supremacy of God in their lives. If Satan could conquer this loyal remnant, his universal dominion would be complete. This is the focus of earth's last battle—the final battle in the great controversy.

Too often, misguided individuals seeking to ascertain the meaning of earth's final events have misinterpreted the prophecies by applying them to the world's latest military conquests. Biblical prophecy, however, always focuses on God's covenant people—literal Israel in Old Testament times; and spiritual Israel, the Christian church, in New Testament times. Scripture is not concerned with political and military events unless they affect the covenant people. The final battle between the king of the north and the king of the south in Daniel 11 has nothing to do with military conquests in the Middle East but everything to do with the battle over the remnant of Revelation 12:17 who keep the commandments of God and have the testimony of Jesus. They are the focal point of the final battle.

In the previous three chapters we have clearly identified the powers involved in this final conflict:

1. The glorious holy mountain is a reference to Mount Zion, or Israel. Israel, in the end-time, represents Christians who are faithful to God. When the king of the north attacks the glorious holy mountain, he is attacking the remnant of Revelation 12:17.

2. The king of the north, while originally referring to God in Daniel 11, refers to the usurper and to those powers that have sought the destruction of the people of God. In 1798, it referred to the medieval papacy. In the last few verses of Daniel 11, it refers to the revitalized religio-political power of the last days that will seek the final destruction of the people of God.

3. The king of the south refers to the French Revolution at the end of the eighteenth century as it introduced an atheistic and secular system of thought which became the dominant philosophy of the world for the next 200 years.

After 200 years of dominance by the king of the south, the world is witnessing the demise of this power. This is exactly what Daniel 11 foretold. Note again verse 40:

> And at the time of the end shall the king of the south push at him: and the king of the north shall come against him like a whirlwind, with chariots, and with horsemen, and with many ships; and he shall enter into the countries, and shall overflow and pass over.

The first part of this verse was dramatically fulfilled when Berthier, Napoleon's general, took the Pope prisoner in 1798. The verse quickly covers the 200 years of dominance by the king of the south and then declares that the king of the north, healed from his deadly wound, would arise, counterattack the king of the south, and destroy him. In fact, verse 40 mentions the king of the south for the last time.

Revelation 13:3 declared that the papacy would receive a deadly wound, that the wound would be healed, and that all the world would wonder after this revived papacy. Daniel 11:40 predicts the same event—the healing of the wound that would eventually develop into the final king of the north.

The healing of the wound began in 1801 with a concordat between Napoleon and the papacy. Soon it renounced its temporal power and aimed for spiritual rather than political control of the world. As a result, it proclaimed the dogma of the universal jurisdiction of the bishop of Rome. That was the beginning. Meanwhile, the world thought the papacy was dead as a political power. While it professed to give up its political aims, it had merely put them on hold, to wait for a more auspicious time.

Political power returned to the papacy in 1929 when the Vatican State was established. Vatican City became a small but significant city-state that was under the control of no government on earth. It was a political power on its own. This was a significant step in the healing of the wound and the reestablishment of the political arm of the papacy. Newspapers reporting on this significant event used the words of Scripture to describe this historic moment.

[Headlines:] Mussolini and Gasparri Sign Historic Roman Pact . . . Heal Wound of Many
Years . . .

Rome, Feb. 11 (AP)—The Roman question tonight was a thing of the past and the Vatican was
at peace with Italy. The formal accomplishment
of this today was the exchange of signatures in
the historic Palace of St. John lateran by two
noteworthy plenipotentiaries, Cardinal Gasparri
for Pope Pius XI and Premier Mussolini for King
Victor Emmanuel III.

In affixing the autographs to the memorable
document, healing the wound which has fes-
tered since 1870, extreme cordiality was dis-
played on both sides. —San Francisco Chronicle,
Tuesday, Feb. 12, 1929, p. 1.

The papacy slowly recovered, from oblivion in
1798, to the recovery of spiritual power in 1870, to
the full restoration of political power in 1929. Today
we are witnessing the reemergence of the papal
system as a dominant world power, respected and
influential. The deadly wound is just about fully
healed. The United States now gives the Vatican
State recognition which it does not give to any other
religious power on earth. During the Reagan years,
the United States voted to send a full ambassador to
Rome to represent United States interests at the Vatican. Today there is regular communication between
the White House and the Vatican.

Rome calling

Pope John Paul II discusses world affairs on the
telephone with George Bush and Mikhail Gorbachev at least once a week, according to Prof.
Malachi Martin, a Roman Catholic theologian

and Vatican insider. . . Martin describes how during the crisis over Lithuania's declaration of independence the Polish-born Pontiff and the embattled Kremlin leader had intense conversations, sometimes several times a day . . . As for his talks with Bush, Martin says the Pope offers the President informed analyses prepared by the Vatican's intelligence network about developments in Eastern Europe and his personal assessments of the new leaders there as well as in the Soviet Union.—*US News and World Report*, August 13, 1990, p. 18.

Within one week of Bill Clinton's election as president of the United States, the media reported that the Vatican had warned him to be careful about how he dealt with moral issues. It appears that the influence will continue.

The power of Rome has reemerged as a major player in the affairs of men, mimicking its leading role during the Middle Ages. Although the papacy in our day does not yet possess the universal persecuting power of the medieval papacy, it will regain that, too, in the final crisis (Revelation 13:3, 15-17).

The complete healing of the wound will take place when the United States erects the image to the beast and enforces the mark of the beast—a religious mark. The Scriptures declare that the entire world will accept this religious mark. If that is so, then at least outwardly there will be no atheist in the final conflict. The king of the south will have been defeated. In order to bring about universal religious agreement, the king of the north must rid the world of atheistic communism and secularism. It has now accomplished the first step—the elimination of communism.

According to Daniel 11:40, it would be this revived papacy, with its wound in the process of being healed, that would attack the king of the south—atheism. Over the last few years we have witnessed the sudden demise of the communist bloc in eastern Europe, and even in that bastion of communism, the Soviet Union. It seems unbelievable that the world could change so quickly and dramatically as it has during the last few years.

Who was responsible for the disintegration of communism? Daniel 11:40 predicted that it would be the revived papacy, and that is exactly what happened. The collapse of communism actually began in Poland with Solidarity; it was because of the influence of Rome that Solidarity was able to gain a foothold in Poland. Most people did not realize that what happened in Poland would very quickly spell doom for communism:

> But the election of John Paul II, a Polish Pope, in 1978 was the signal event. When he visited Poland in 1979, six million of his countrymen, a sixth of the population, turned out to see him. He proclaimed Christianity and communism incompatible. The church became the center of political protest in Poland.

> With the Pope's support, Solidarity was formed, and John Paul II sent word to Moscow that if Soviet forces crushed Solidarity, he would go to Poland and stand with his people. The Soviets were so alarmed they hatched a plot to kill him. In 1981 the Pope was shot by a professional killer in St. Peter's Square, miraculously he survived.—"Communism's Incredible Collapse: How It Happened" by Fred Barnes. *Reader's Digest*, March 1990.

Incredible! Exactly as Daniel 11:40 predicted, the king of the south was defeated by the king of the north. What is so astonishing is the rapidity with which the downfall came—so fast that most of us stood bewildered before our television screens not believing what we saw happening before our eyes. Interestingly, Daniel 11:40 even predicted the rapidity of its downfall. "The king of the north shall come against him like a whirlwind" (verse 40, KJV). Indeed, it appeared like a mighty whirlwind as communism fell in different nations like dominos.

Time magazine published an article on the current debate about the Virgin Mary in the Catholic church. One of the fascinating revelations in this article was the following statement germane to the question of who caused the fall of communism:

> John Paul is firmly convinced ... that Mary brought an end to communism throughout Europe ... The Virgin predicted the rise of Soviet totalitarianism before it happened. In a subsequent vision, she directed the Pope and his bishops to consecrate Russia to her Immaculate Heart in order to bring communism to an end. ...
>
> John Paul . . . carried out Mary's directive correctly in 1984—and the very next year Mikhail Gorbachev's rise to power inaugurated the Soviet collapse. Says Father Robert Fox of the Fatima Family Shrine in Alexandria, South Dakota: "The world will recognize in due time that the defeat of communism came at the intercession of the mother of Jesus."—"Handmaid or Feminist," *Time*, Dec. 30, 1991, pp. 64, 65.

In reality, the downfall of communism was not accomplished by Rome alone. She had a very active partner—President Reagan.

> On June 7, 1982, Reagan and John Paul met for fifty minutes at the Vatican. During that conversation the plot was hatched to eliminate communism.
>
> In that meeting, Reagan and the Pope agreed to undertake a clandestine campaign to hasten the dissolution of the communist empire. Declares Richard Allen, Reagan's first National Security Adviser: "This was one of the great secret alliances of all time."—Time, February 24, 1992, "The Holy Alliance," p. 28.

Time magazine's cover for the week of February 24, 1992 featured this amazing story of the plot to eliminate communism hatched by Reagan and John Paul. The cover read: "HOLY ALLIANCE. How Reagan and the Pope conspired to assist Poland's Solidarity movement and hasten the demise of Communism." Note some of the fascinating revelations from this article in *Time*:

> Until Solidarity's legal status was restored in 1989 it flourished underground, supplied, nurtured and advised largely by the network established under the auspices of Reagan and John Paul II. Tons of equipment—fax machines (the first in Poland), printing presses, transmitters, telephones, shortwave radios, video cameras, photocopiers, telex machines, computers, word processors—were smuggled into Poland via channels established by priests and American agents and representatives of the AFL-CIO and European labor movements.—*Ibid.*
>
> The key Administration players were all devout Roman Catholics—CIA chief William Casey, Allen, Clark, Haig, Walters and William Wilson, Reagan's first ambassador to the Vatican. They

regarded the U.S.-Vatican relationship as a holy alliance: the moral force of the Pope and the teachings of their church combined with their fierce anticommunism and their notion of American democracy. Yet the mission would have been impossible without the full support of Reagan, who believed fervently in both the benefits and the practical applications of Washington's relationship with the Vatican. One of the earliest goals as President, Reagan says, was to recognize the Vatican as a state "and make them an ally."—*Ibid*, p. 31.

"Nobody believed the collapse of communism would happen this fast on this timetable," says a cardinal who is one of the Pope's closest aides. "But in their first meeting, the Holy Father and the president committed themselves and the institutions of the church and America to such a goal. And from that day, the focus was to bring it about in Poland."—*Ibid*, p. 35.

Even Mikhail Gorbachev recognized the role the Pope had played in the downfall of Eastern Europe:

Now it can be said that everything which took place in Eastern Europe in recent years would have been impossible without the Pope's efforts and the enormous role, including the political role, which he played in the world arena.

Pope John Paul II will play an enormous political role now that profound changes have occurred in European history."—*Toronto Star*, Toronto, Ontario, Canada, March 9, 1992, article by Mikhail Gorbachev.

There can be no doubt that the recent demise of the Soviet empire was the direct result of the reemergence of the Pope as a major political force in the world. Communism appears to be dead, but Rome has emerged from the rubbish heap of communism as one of the dominant world players.

Even more fascinating is what is happening in these countries in the aftermath of communism's demise. Many have lauded the freedoms that have come, but are these countries really free, or has one totalitarianism been replaced with another—religious totalitarianism?

> WARSAW (Reuters)—Poland's powerful Roman Catholic bishops—reaching for more influence, especially in their fight against abortion—said Thursday the separation of church and state should be abolished in the former communist country. . . .

> "The formula separating the Catholic church from the state should be removed from the constitution," the bishops said in a statement.

> Ending the separation enshrined in the former communist constitution would make Catholicism the state religion. . . .

> The church, the strongest ally of Solidarity during its fight to topple communism, has increased its political influence since the trade-union movement won power in 1989. . . .

> It has called the present liberal law, introduced under communism, "an ally of evil."

> The bishops' initiatives have provoked a growing debate on the role of the church in post-communist Poland.

> "Before, people were afraid of the party. Now they are afraid of the church," a critic said.—*Chicago Tribune*, April 26, 1991, Section 1, p. 18.

As communism disappears from the lands of eastern Europe, the Roman church has been moving in, replacing the communist political power. Based on history, believers may have more to fear from the religious intolerance of Romanism than they did from the secular intolerance of communism.

Not only is Rome having an impact on the former communist lands, she also impacting America and its policies. In the new world that has arisen since the demise of communism, Pope John Paul II is seriously influencing even American foreign policy. The area of its impact is in the furtherance of the church's teachings. *Time* magazine also revealed this penetrating view of the influence of the Papal See:

> In response to concerns of the Vatican, the Reagan Administration agreed to alter its foreign aid program to comply with the church's teachings on birth control.—*Time*, "The U.S. and the Vatican on Birth Control," February 24, 1992, p. 35.

Amazingly, America is now bowing in humble obeisance to the wishes of the Pope. Alliance with Rome comes with a price to America. America must comply with the church's teachings on birth control in her foreign aid. One can only wonder how long it will be before the Pope will insist on America complying with other religious dogmas.

What are the aims of the papacy today? Exactly the same as they were in the Middle Ages—the total domination of the world. Roman Catholic scholar and former Vatican insider, Malachi Martin, in his recent book *The Keys of This Blood*, wrote this as the subtitle of the book: "Pope John Paul II versus Russia and the West for Control of the New World Order."

Make no mistake about it—the aims of the papacy remain unchanged. She has already conquered Russia. According to Martin, only the West, led by the United States, remains to be conquered. Even now we see the United States courting the Roman pontiff. How will the papacy conquer America? America will simply join with the papacy. That's the subject of the next chapter, as we look at Revelation 13.

What are the aims of the present Pope—John Paul II? Malachi Martin leaves us in no doubt as to the geopolitical nature of the current pontiff. What he says is astounding to students of Bible prophecy:

> In the final analysis, John Paul II is a geopolitician-pope who spent the first part of his pontificate establishing himself and his Holy See as authentic players in the millennium endgame, which, during the same period of time, has become the "only game in town" and in this last decade of the second millennium will absorb the energies, the efforts and the vital interests of the great powers in our world.—Malachi Martin, *The Keys of this Blood*, pp. 638, 639.

> He is waiting, rather, for an event that will fission human history, splitting the immediate past from the oncoming future. It will be an event on public view in the skies, in the oceans, and on the continental landmasses of this planet. It will particularly involve our human sun, which every day lights up and shines upon the valleys, the mountains and the plains of this earth for our eyes. But on the day of this event, it will not

appear merely as the master star of our so-called solar system. Rather, it will be seen as the circumambient glory of the Woman whom the apostle describes as "clothed with the sun" and giving birth to "a child who will rule the nations with a scepter of iron."

Fissioning it will be as an event, in John Paul's conviction of faith, for it will immediately nullify all the grand designs the nations are now forming and will introduce the Grand Design of man's Maker. John Paul's waiting and watching time will then be over. His ministry as the Servant of the Grand Design will then begin. His strength of will to hold on and continue, and then, when the fissioning event occurs, to assume that ministry, derives directly from the Petrine authority entrusted solely to him the day he became Pope, in October of 1978. That authority, that strength, is symbolized in the Keys of Peter, washed in the human blood of the God-Man, Jesus Christ. John Paul is and will be the sole possessor of the Keys of this Blood on that day.—*Ibid*, p. 639.

What Martin declares here is that some supernatural event will occur within the decade of the 90s that will cause the whole world to reject its present order of secular thinking. The Pope will then emerge as the one world leader who can restore the new world order—an order in which religion is once again in control of society, as it was in the Middle Ages. In the interval, while the Pope waits for this event, he has engineered the collapse of communism. This begins with a reunited Europe under the Pope's control.

What Europe has that makes it a focal point in modern history and development is its tradition.

It was the cradle and the luxuriant garden of what is called Western civilization. From Europe came the philosophy, the law, the literature, and the science that have gone into the makeup of our modernity. Europe's influence is still enormous in its potential. Besides all that, for over forty-five years Europe has been divided in two, the Eastern half housing an ideology and a sociopolitical system that constantly threatened the rest of the world.—*Ibid.*, p. 652.

The Pope realizes that the foundation of a truly united Europe is Catholicism. Yet the Pope delays forcing this issue, except in his beloved Poland. Once the supernatural sign occurs, he will govern not only Europe, but the whole world. That's why he waits patiently. But that is his game plan. Notice as Martin continues his illuminating picture:

In these circumstances, John Paul's lament is understandable. Europe's origins, its rise to power, its contributions to civilization, its glories, all were marinated in Roman Christianity. In fact, Europe became Europe under the close tutelage of the Roman popes. Its tradition was thoroughly Christian. "Europe," Hilaire Belloc wrote, "was the Faith. The Faith was Europe." That tradition of profound moral, spiritual, and intellectual excellence was built on the power and according to the laws of Europe's Christian origins.—*Ibid*, pp. 652, 653.

Don't miss Martin's penetrating insight into Pope John Paul II. His aim is a united Europe under his control. To accomplish this he must destroy both communism and the secularism of the West—

the king of the south. He is halfway to his goal. The end of the West will occur by some great supernatural event.

That is why John Paul is waiting. God must first intervene, before John Paul's major ministry to all men can start.

> In Papa Wojtyla's outlook, therefore, the Grand Design of which he is the nominated Servant is the design of divine providence to recall men to the values that derive only from belief, from religion and from divine revelation. His is an unpleasant message and, for the moment, a thankless job. He has to warn his contemporaries of his conviction that human catastrophe on a world scale—according to his information—is impending.

> He has to admit that he, like everybody else, is in the dark as to when it will occur, although he does know some of the horrific details of that worldwide catastrophe. He knows also that it will not come without prior warning, but that only those already renewed in heart—and that would probably be a minority—will recognize it for what it is and make preparation for the tribulations that will follow.

> He also knows that these will start unexpectedly and be accompanied by overall confusion of minds and darkening of human understanding, and will result in the shattering of any plans for a "greater European space" and the mega-market plans for "greater Europe" and the "Pacific Rim." It will be the death and entombment of Leninist Marxism and the effective liquidation of the long—centuries long—war that the forces of this civilized world have waged against the Church Christ founded and the religious belief of that

Church. The battle between the Gospel and the anti-Gospel will be over. The other two major contenders in the millennium endgame will be eliminated.—*Ibid*, pp. 656, 657.

Note especially the last sentence in Martin's assessment. The New World Order will be dominated by a Roman Pope who will have defeated the two contenders for world power—Russia and the West. This seems to be such an accurate fulfillment of Daniel 11:40 that one can only wonder at how quickly the rest of Daniel 11 will be fulfilled.

What is the supernatural sign from the heavens that John Paul II is looking for? One can only speculate. The Bible clearly tells us that supernatural signs and wonders will take place in the last days and will deceive many.

For there shall arise false Christs, and false prophets, and shall shew great signs and wonders; insomuch that, if it were possible, they shall deceive the very elect. (Matthew 24:24.)

And he doeth great wonders, so that he maketh fire come down from heaven on the earth in the sight of men, And deceiveth them that dwell on the earth by the means of those miracles which he had power to do in the sight of the beast; saying to them that dwell on the earth, that they should make an image to the beast, which had the wound by a sword, and did live. (Revelation 13:13, 14.)

And I saw three unclean spirits like frogs come out of the mouth of the dragon, and out of the mouth of the beast, and out of the mouth of the false prophet. For they are the spirits of devils, working miracles, which go forth unto the kings of the earth and of the whole world, to gather them to the battle of that great day of God Almighty. (Revelation 16:13, 14.)

This reminds me of another penetrating prophetic insight written over 100 years ago. In speaking of the horrific final scenes of earth's history, the writer describes Satan's impersonation of the second coming of Christ.

As the crowning act in the great drama of deception, Satan himself will personate Christ. The church has long professed to look to the Saviour's advent as the consummation of her hopes. Now the great deceiver will make it appear that Christ has come. In different parts of the earth, Satan will manifest himself among men as a majestic being of dazzling brightness, resembling the description of the Son of God given by John in the Revelation. Revelation 1:13-15. The glory that surrounds him is unsurpassed by anything that mortal eyes have yet beheld. The shout of triumph rings out upon the air: "Christ has come! Christ has come!" The people prostrate themselves in adoration before him, while he lifts up his hands and pronounces a blessing upon them, as Christ blessed His disciples when He was upon the earth. His voice is soft and subdued, yet full of melody. In gentle, compassionate tones he presents some of the same gracious, heavenly truths which the Saviour uttered; he heals the diseases of the people. . . . This is the strong almost overmastering delusion.—E. G. White, *The Great Controversy*, p. 624.

Could this be what the Pope is waiting for? Certainly a majestic impersonation of Christ's return would give tremendous credence to the emergence of John Paul's new world order. The Pope's information about the coming event has been received through the visions of the Virgin Mary to a girl at Fatima.

Having destroyed communism and the secularism of the West, the king of the north who has now reemerged in great power, will be united with yet another major power in the last days. That power is revealed in Revelation 13 and is the subject of the next chapter. But notice what this renewed king of the north does after he destroys the king of the south:

> And at the time of the end shall the king of the south push at him: and the king of the north shall come against him like a whirlwind, with chariots, and with horsemen, and with many ships; and he shall enter into the countries, and shall overflow and pass over. He shall stretch forth his hand also upon the countries: and the land of Egypt shall not escape. But he shall have power over the treasures of gold and of silver, and over all the precious things of Egypt; and the Libyans and the Ethiopians shall be at his steps. But tidings out of the east and out of the north shall trouble him: therefore he shall go forth with great fury to destroy, and utterly to make away many. And he shall plant the tabernacles of his palace between the seas in the glorious holy mountain; yet he shall come to his end, and none shall help him.

> And at that time shall Michael stand up, the great prince which standeth for the children of thy people: and there shall be a time of trouble, such as never was since there was a nation even to that same time: and at that time thy people shall be delivered, every one that shall be found written in the book. (Daniel 11:40-12:1.)

Amazingly, this revived king of the north, having destroyed the king of the south, will launch his final attack against the people of the covenant. It is those who are faithful to the Scriptures and to the Lord Jesus Christ who will undergo the fiercest onslaught by this final enemy of God's people. He will come at them with "great rage" (Daniel 11:44). Revelation 12:17 declares that he "was enraged at the woman and went off to make war against the rest of her offspring." The focal point of this final battle is the remnant of the woman—the faithful disciples of Christ at the end time.

We will examine this battle in greater detail in a subsequent chapter. Note now, however, in unmistakable terms, that God delivers His people and wins this battle. We know the outcome. The final king of the north may appear to be dominant, but he will lose as Christ enters the arena and rings down the curtain on Planet Earth. O glorious day! May it come soon. The events of the last few years indicate clearly that we are approaching this final moment when the revived king of the north once again becomes dominant in the new world order.

On the surface it may appear as if the Pope himself will be the sole ruler in this final conflict, yet Revelation 13 adds a significant new detail to the scenario. Another world power that is destined to join forces with this revived Romanism emerges on the religious scene, and under this union, the final crisis will come to God's people. Let's turn now to Revelation 13 and discover this fascinating new development.

OVERVIEW OF DANIEL'S PROPHECIES

Daniel 2	Daniel 7	Daniel 8-9	Daniel 10-12	Interpretation
Head of gold	Lion			Babylon
Breast and arms of silver	Bear	Ram	3 kings	Medo-Persia
Belly and thighs of brass	Leopard	He-goat	Mighty king	Greece
	4 Heads of leopard	4 horns	King of north and south	Divisions of Greece
Legs of iron	Dragon	Little horn	King of North	Rome
Feet of iron and clay	10 horns			Divisions of Rome
	Little horn	Little horn	King of North	Papacy
	Judgment	Sanctuary cleansed		Judgment
			Final conflict involving King of the North	Revived Papal/ Protestant/ Spiritualistic Union—Spiritual Babylon
Stone smashes image	Kingdom given to saints	Desolations to the end	God's people delivered	Second coming of Christ

8

America Takes the Lead

What is at stake in the present conflict shaping up in our world? Clearly, it is the ultimate control of the world. Each of the various forces wants to be in control of the new world order that is developing after the demise of atheistic communism. Already we see that Pope John Paul II has taken the credit for the fall of communism. President Bush has claimed that he and President Reagan were responsible for the collapse of communism. What many have not realized was the fact that the Pope and the President may have been acting together in the creation of this new world order. While this fact has not been publicized until recently, it is now clear that there was a secret plot between the Pope and Reagan to destroy communism (see previous chapter).

With communism defeated, the Pope can focus on conquering the capitalist West so that his dominion will once again be universal. This is the intention of the Pope, according to Vatican insider Malachi Martin in his book, *The Keys of This Blood*. The subtitle on the inside of the book is most intriguing: "The Struggle for World Dominion Between Pope John Paul II, Mikhail Gorbachev, and the Capitalist West." With Mikhail Gorbachev out of the picture in 1992, the center of attention now shifts to the capitalist West. Amazingly, Bible prophecy forecasts a major role for the United States in this final conflict: to bring America and the world back to allegiance to Rome. This may well be the path that both Rome and America wish. Prophecy makes clear that Rome does not conquer America, but America joins hands with Romanism, crossing the gulf created 500 years ago by the Reformation. When that happens, we will have seen the creation of a new world order—one which is totally different from what many people have dreamed it would be. It will be a world order dominated by Rome and religion. This amazing prophecy is captured for us in Revelation 13.

The First Beast of Revelation 13

Revelation 13:1-10 describes a beast that is to arise out of the sea. As we examine its identifying marks, it is clear that this beast is the same power that the prophet Daniel portrayed in Daniel 7. Daniel called it the little horn, and it represented the Roman Church with its union of church and state during the Dark Ages. Let's note its identifying marks in Revelation:

CRAIG ROBINSON, ARTIST

"And I stood upon the sand of the sea, and saw a
beast rise up out of the sea, having seven heads
and ten horns . . ."
—*Revelation 13:1*

1. The beast dominated western Europe after the breakup of the Roman Empire (verses 1, 2).

> And I stood upon the sand of the sea, and saw a beast rise up out of the sea, having seven heads and ten horns, and upon his horns ten crowns, and upon his heads the name of blasphemy. And the beast which I saw was like unto a leopard, and his feet were as the feet of a bear, and his mouth as the mouth of a lion: and the dragon gave him his power, and his seat, and great authority. (Revelation 13:1, 2.)

The ten crowns on his heads clearly represent the kingly power exercised by the bishop of Rome over the ten divisions of the Roman empire. The lion, bear, leopard, and dragon symbols are all borrowed from Daniel 7, indicating that the beast of Revelation 13 is a continuation of those powers that had dominated Europe for the past 1,000 years. Its power, indeed, came from the fourth beast—the dragon—who gave the bishop of Rome his power, seat, and great authority, so that in the Roman see, we have the continuation of the old pagan Roman empire.

2. Romanism received a deadly wound in 1798 that eventually would be healed (verse 3).

> And I saw one of his heads as it were wounded to death; and his deadly wound was healed: and all the world wondered after the beast. (Revelation 13:3.)

As previously observed, the fatal wound was received in 1798 when Berthier, the French general under Napoleon, invaded the Vatican and took the Pope prisoner. Since 1860, we have witnessed the gradual healing of the wound, with a major healing occurring in 1929 when Mussolini restored the Pope to the Vatican as a secular ruler. Today, just as predicted, we are witnessing a total resurrection of the political arm of the papacy with its aspirations of total world dominance.

3. It is a religious power which receives worship (verse 4).

And they worshipped the dragon which gave power unto the beast: and they worshipped the beast, saying, Who is like unto the beast? who is able to make war with him? (Revelation 13:4.)

There is no question that the Roman power is a religious power, which receives the veneration and worship of its followers.

4. It is a blasphemous power that ruled for 1260 years (verses 5, 6).

And there was given unto him a mouth speaking great things and blasphemies; and power was given unto him to continue forty and two months. And he opened his mouth in blasphemy against God, to blaspheme his name, and his tabernacle, and them that dwell in heaven. (Revelation 13:5, 6.)

The blasphemous nature of the papacy was clearly shown in our study of Daniel 7. His claim to forgive sins, change laws, and to be equal to God leaves no doubt as to the blasphemous nature of this power, especially as it exercised world dominion during the Dark Ages. For exactly 1260 years (the forty-two months of verse 5), the papacy exercised political power. These 1260 years of papal political domination extended from A.D. 538, when the decree of Justinian took effect, until 1798, when Berthier removed the Pope from the Vatican, effectively ending his political power.

5. It was a persecuting power (verse 7).

> And it was given unto him to make war with the saints, and to overcome them: and power was given him over all kindreds, and tongues, and nations. (Revelation 13:7.)

The fifty million people who died in Europe as a result of the persecuting nature of this power would have had little doubt that the papacy of the Dark Ages indeed made war with God's saints. He maintained control over all of these nations because of his persecuting nature, which was feared and dreaded by the populace.

A historian recounting this terrible period of persecution remarks:

> "That the Church of Rome has shed more innocent blood than any other institution that has ever existed among mankind, will be questioned by no Protestant who has a competent knowledge of history . . .

> "The number of those who were put to death for their religion in the Netherlands alone, in the reign of Charles V, has been estimated by a very high authority at 50,000, and at least half as many perished under his son."—W.E.H. Lecky, *History of the Rise and Influence of the Spirit of Rationalism in Europe* (reprint: New York: Braziller, 1955), Vol. 2, pp. 40, 41.

6. The whole world acknowledges his supremacy (verse 8).

> And all that dwell upon the earth shall worship him, whose names are not written in the book of life of the Lamb slain from the foundation of the world. (Revelation 13:8.)

During the 1260-year reign, few challenged the universal dominion and control of the church over both the religious and the secular interests of the world.

These six marks of identification from Revelation 13 make it clear that the power here spoken of is none other than the papal system during the Middle Ages. The only power which arose to dominate Europe during this time was Rome. It has exactly fulfilled all the specifications of the prophecy.

The purpose of this chapter is not to deal again with the rise of medieval Catholicism—we have already covered that in a previous chapter. Here we will simply review the setting for the tremendous revelation about to be given in the second half of Chapter 13.

In order to fully understand the implications of this second beast in Revelation 13, however, one must clearly understand the identity of the first beast. The first beast is the Roman Church of the Dark Ages, which ruled the world with an iron fist, united church and state, and claimed universal dominion over the minds and souls of all people. The second beast is to bring a revival of medieval Romanism to the world at the end of the twentieth century.

The Second Beast of Revelation 13

If any man have an ear, let him hear. He that leadeth into captivity shall go into captivity: he that killeth with the sword must be killed with the sword. Here is the patience and the faith of the saints. And I beheld another beast coming up out of the earth; and he had two horns like a lamb, and he spake as a dragon. (Revelation 13:9-11.)

Here emerges another beast, which initially is not as ferocious as the first beast. (A beast is symbolic of a kingdom or power. See Daniel 7:23.) The second beast has three identifying marks:

1. The second beast comes into power around 1798. Verse 8 indicates that the first beast is going into captivity just before the second beast arises. Since the first beast (Romanism) goes *into* captivity in 1798, we could expect the second beast to be rising to prominence around 1798.

2. The second beast rises in a new country. All other beasts arose out of the sea; the second beast is the only one to arise out of the earth. Since the sea is symbolic of population (Revelation 17:15), the earth, being the opposite of the sea, would be symbolic of a land without heavy population. This beast, then, does not arise by military conquest of the lands of Europe, as all other beasts have, but instead arises in a new land.

3. The second beast is characterized as lamb-like—innocent and freedom-loving. While other beasts in Daniel and Revelation were very ferocious, this beast is lamblike in its inception. This power is not seeking world dominion when it arises. Thus it is totally different in character from the beasts that have preceded it.

These three marks of identification make clear that the second beast is a reference to the rise of the United States of America. Arising out of the Revolutionary War in the latter part of the eighteenth century, the United States was coming into its own around 1798, at the same time the first beast was going into captivity. The United States was born, not in Europe, but on a new continent. It did not

HARRY ANDERSON, ARTIST

"And I beheld another beast coming up out of
the earth; and he had two horns like a lamb, and
he spake like a dragon."
—*Revelation 13:11*

conquer Europe; rather, it fought a war to be separate from Europe—to develop its own destiny. For most of its existence the United States was a non-domineering power in the world. It did not seek control of other nations, but instead sought a peaceful co-existence. It was indeed like a lamb at its inception.

The United States differed from previous world governments, which had always sought to unite the church and the state. In America a new experiment evolved—a separation of church and state. All religions were free to espouse their beliefs, win converts, and practice their religion with no interference from the state, and people were free to practice no religion if that was their choice. It is this separation of church and state that makes the United States different in the prophetic picture. If the separation of church and state were lost, America would revert back to being the same kind of power that has always dominated the world.

America's unique destiny was to create a world where people were not coerced into religion by fear of the state, but could choose any religion or no religion based on their conscience alone. Thank God for the great role that America has played for nearly 200 years!

This is not, however, the final picture of America. As chapter 13 of Revelation continues, it declares that the lamb-like beast would eventually speak as a dragon. To speak as a dragon is to persecute those who dissent (Revelation 12:13). In order to fulfill this prediction, America will need to repudiate her constitution and the bill of rights, which guarantee freedom of religion and the separation of church and state. In doing so, America will lose her unique role in human history. Yet this is the inevitable future of the United States as foreseen by John the Revelator:

> And I beheld another beast coming up out of the earth; and he had two horns like a lamb, and he spake as a dragon. And he exerciseth all the power of the first beast before him, and causeth the earth and them which dwell therein to worship the first beast, whose deadly wound was healed.
>
> And he doeth great wonders, so that he maketh fire come down from heaven on the earth in the sight of men. And deceiveth them that dwell on the earth by the means of those miracles which he had power to do in the sight of the beast; saying to them that dwell on the earth, that they should make an image to the beast, which had the wound by a sword, and did live. And he had power to give life unto the image of the beast, that the image of the beast should both speak, and cause that as many as would not worship the image of the beast should be killed. And he causeth all, both small and great, rich and poor, free and bond, to receive a mark in their right hand, or in their foreheads: And that no man might buy or sell, save he that had the mark, or the name of the beast, or the number of his name. (Revelation 13:11-17.)

Amazing! America takes the lead in causing the entire world to worship the first beast, whose fatal wound had been healed. Note that this prophetic role of the United States is not exercised until the fatal wound is completely healed and the first beast, Romanism, has once again emerged on the world scene as a major power.

America's Prophetic Role

As we noted in the previous chapter, the revived king of the north has arisen. Pope John Paul II has led his papacy to such global heights that he is the renowned confidant of all world leaders.

With the demise of communism, the United States has emerged as the one remaining superpower. For the first time in its history, the United States is poised to assume its destined role as the undisputed leader of the world. This leadership, Scripture declares, will ultimately bring the entire world into the camp of Rome once again. It is America who will take the lead in causing the world once again to worship at the shrine of Rome. One prophetic writer, sensing the impact of Revelation 13, describes the events we are watching unfold in our world today in these prophetic words:

> The Protestants of the United States will be foremost in stretching their hands across the gulf to grasp the hand of spiritualism; they will reach over the abyss to clasp hands with the Roman power; and under the influence of this threefold union, this country will follow in the steps of Rome in trampling on the rights of conscience.— E. G. White, *The Great Controversy*, p. 588.

What used to be known as Protestant America will be foremost in paving the way for the reestablishment of the medieval papacy. When that has happened, all the events foretold in Revelation 13 will be speedily fulfilled.

In past decades it has seemed almost inconceivable that America could ever fulfill Revelation 13. How could America become such a dominant power that the whole world would follow her example? Communism stood in the way. But now communism is gone, and America is poised to fulfill her prophetic role.

Not only does Revelation 13 predict that America will lead the world back to Rome; it also predicts how the United States will eliminate the separation of church and state. Revelation 13:13, 14 declares that to bring about these sweeping changes, America will witness a revival of supernatural power. Miraculous signs, wonders, and healings will occur. These amazing signs will awaken the United States to the feeling that God is leading in this union with Rome. The people will be deceived through the miracles, and all the world will bow in humble obeisance to the new world order.

In the previous chapter we learned that Pope John Paul II is waiting for some kind of supernatural sign that will send the world to his feet as the only leader of the new world order. Revelation 13 predicts that those signs—even fire falling from heaven—will occur in America (verse 13). In Scripture, fire falling from heaven has always been proof that God was with the movement. In the Old Testament, fire falling down on Mount Carmel proved that Elijah's message was from God. The failure of the prophets of Baal to produce fire indicated that they were not of God.

Fire in the New Testament symbolizes the presence of the Holy Spirit. The seven lamps of fire burning before the throne of God, as described in Revelation 4:5, is interpreted to be a symbol of the perfect Holy Spirit. John the Baptist predicted that

Christ would baptize with the Holy Spirit and with fire (Matthew 3:11; Luke 3:16).

It is not surprising, then, to discover that in the last great deception, Satan brings down fire from heaven to support the direction that the United States is taking in bringing the world to Rome. Revelation 13 predicts that a counterfeit revival will follow, which will be accompanied by a false Holy Spirit. Those promoting the false revival will claim that God is with them because of the presence of the Holy Spirit, as proved by the miracle of the fire. As a result of the false revival, America will be led to erect an image of the beast (Revelation 13:14). The tragedy is that most Americans will be deceived by this counterfeit revival.

Scripture indicates that there is a particular form the Holy Spirit takes when it is symbolized by fire. Acts 2:3, 4 describes the genuine outpouring of the Holy Spirit on the day of Pentecost. Notice the description of this event:

> And when the day of Pentecost was fully come, they were all with one accord in one place. And suddenly there came a sound from heaven as of a rushing mighty wind, and it filled all the house where they were sitting. And there appeared unto them cloven tongues like as of fire, and it sat upon each of them. And they were all filled with the Holy Ghost, and began to speak with other tongues, as the Spirit gave them utterance. (Acts 2:1-4.)

Interestingly, Scripture links the falling of the Holy Spirit to fire and the gift of tongues. Under this false revivalistic movement, great signs, miracles, and wonders will be produced, all calculated to create a great following among the people. Miracles and the false gift of tongues will be accepted in place of God's truth. Yet this is a false revival because it is grounded on a false authority—miracles, not Scripture.

The Gift of Tongues

Yet a genuine gift of tongues is taught in Scripture—one that can still be manifested today. That is the gift of known languages used to communicate the gospel to those who do not understand the language used by the proclaimer. This is the same gift written about in the Book of Acts. It was understood by those who heard it—or if it wasn't, someone always interpreted.

Tongues-speaking in the early church was regarded as the least of the spiritual gifts and was never regarded as an absolute necessity for every believer (1 Corinthians 12:28-31). Scripture is clear that it was not a requirement that everyone speak in tongues as a spiritual sign that they were born again or baptized by the Spirit. Yet that is what many modern tongues exponents claim. Jesus did not speak in tongues, but never was there one so baptized of the Spirit as He. Paul cautioned against an undue emphasis on the gift of tongues in 1 Corinthians 14:22, 23 (NKJV):

> Therefore tongues are for a sign, not to those who believe but to unbelievers; but prophesying is not for unbelievers but for those who believe. Therefore if the whole church comes together in one place, and all speak with tongues, and there come in those who are uninformed or unbelievers, will they not say that you are out of your mind?

The biblical gift of tongues was to communicate

the gospel to unbelievers. Therefore, it was not to be practiced in the church as an exercise in spiritual superiority. Such a demonstration might cause unbelievers to assume that such Christians were unbalanced mentally. Yet much of the modern usage of this gift tends to resemble that which the apostle Paul warned against, rather than the biblical gift of languages to communicate the gospel.

The work of the Holy Spirit is to lead people into God's truth. His Word is truth:

> Howbeit when he, the Spirit of truth, is come, he will guide you into all truth: for he shall not speak of himself; but whatsoever he shall hear, that shall he speak: and he will shew you things to come. He shall glorify me: for he shall receive of mine, and shall shew it unto you. (John 16:13, 14.)

A genuine baptism of the Holy Spirit will lead people to acknowledge biblical truth and will glorify Jesus. The Holy Spirit does not talk about Himself, but He exalts Jesus. We need to be leery of a spirit that is always calling attention to itself. Only the spirit of Lucifer does that (Isaiah 14:13). The genuine Holy Spirit is always talking about Jesus.

There are genuine miracles, healings, signs, and tongues operating in these last days, but they can never be used as an excuse for not following the clearly revealed Word of God in Scripture. Remember that the devil also is performing miracles and signs as part of this final great deception (Revelation 13:13, 14). The true evidence of Spirit possession is not in the outward physical phenomena of shouting, dancing, falling prostrate, or speaking in tongues—nor even in miracles. The true evidence of the indwelling of the Holy Spirit is seen in the fruit of the Spirit in the lives of transformed individuals (Galatians 5:22, 23). Love, joy, and peace in the life are the biblical signs of the baptism of the Holy Spirit—not outward physical phenomena.

The Rise of the False Revival in America

This false miracle-working power and false use of the gift of tongues will eventually become world-wide and will deceive nearly the whole world. There are good, sincere people involved in this movement, just as there were sincere people when Romanism dominated the church of the Dark Ages. Yet that does not make the movement biblically right.

Revelation 13:13-15 foresees the time when this false revival will become nearly universal and will give life, or power, to the papacy. Remember that John Paul II is waiting for a supernatural sign. The church, so formal and dead, will suddenly be revived by this infusion of false power.

In the summer of 1967, the tongues movement invaded the Roman church at Notre Dame University when many priests, nuns, and laypeople supposedly received the Holy Spirit and spoke in tongues. From there it spread throughout Romanism, until today it has become a major force in the Roman Church. It has also jumped denominational lines and invaded Protestantism. It is no longer relegated to the "holy rollers," but has now entered mainstream Protestantism and has achieved acceptability. In fact, it has become the great unifying factor in Christendom today. Where attempts to formally unite all the denominations have failed, the charismatic movement has united Christians as nothing else could.

Who is the source of this modern movement? According to Revelation 13:13, 14, it is Satan's masterpiece of deception to deceive the world into returning to the camp of Rome. The tongues, miracles, signs, and wonders are all of a supernatural character, with links to spiritualism. Remember, spiritualism is what is to unite America with Rome, bridging the gulf to create the threefold union of the final king of the north. Note the following comparisons between Roger Alexander, who describes his experience in speaking in tongues with a Spirit medium and a popular faith healer.

> As my friends began to pray over me, I felt a strange physical sensation start in my hands and feet, and gradually spread over my whole body. It was like an electrical current or as though the inside of my body were shaking against my skin.—Roger Alexander, "The Holy Spirit at Michigan State," *Acts, Today's News of the Holy Spirit's Renewal*, Sept.-Oct. 1967, p. 23.

> In entering the trance condition, your hands and body may twist and jerk, as if you were being treated to a series of galvanic shocks. When the spirit enters, in the arms are felt peculiar tingling sensations like needles and pins, something akin to a current of electricity passing through from head to foot.—Spiritist medium Vishita, Bhakta Swami, *Genuine Mediumship*, Chas. T. Powner, Publisher, Chicago, 1941, p. 37.

> I felt physical contact with God's presence in my right hand. It was a tingling sensation like an electric current. I felt a strange and glorious sen-

sation like an electrical current flowing through my hands. It seemed like 10,000 volts of electricity were passing through my body.—Faith healer Oral Roberts, *Life Story*, p. 110.

One who had formerly been involved in tongues speaking, now speaks frankly about the source of some of the tongues speaking with which he is acquainted:

"But", someone might ask, "didn't the interpretation of the tongues benefit the church?" To answer that, let me tell a couple of incidents with which I am personally familiar. In one meeting I was in, a certain person spoke in a tongue and another gave the interpretation. Then a third person stood up, a visitor. He said, "I am a Jew. I have heard of this gift of tongues and I came to see what it was all about. That was Hebrew that that person was speaking, but he was not praising God as the so-called interpreter said he was doing. Instead, he was cursing God.

On another occasion when I was present, a local member gave an utterance, and he was interpreted as saying, "I am God, give me your worship and praise." But there was a couple visiting that night from New York. The man stood and introduced himself. He said, "I have visited Pentecostal meetings several times, but I have never before heard anyone speaking in tongues. I came tonight because I wanted to hear what it was like. I am Italian, and that message was in Italian. But instead of 'I am God,' as the interpreter said, the message actually was, 'I am Satan—I am your lord and master.'"—James Beshires, Jr. *Praise the Lord*, pp. 108, 109.

Bible-believing Christians need to be very cautious of any movement with such a heavy emphasis on the supernatural, especially in light of the prediction of Revelation 13. We have witnessed the birth of the movement that will perhaps usher in the power that will bring America and the world back to Rome. Scripture is clear—there will be supernatural signs, tongues, and miracles that will accompany the movement to erect the image to the beast.

The Image of the Beast

Because of the signs he was given power to do on behalf of the first beast, he deceived the inhabitants of the earth. He ordered them to set up an image in honor of the beast who was wounded by the sword and yet lived. (Revelation 13:14, NIV.)

Note again that it is the performance of the miracles and signs that gives America the power to erect the image of the beast. The deceived people of America willingly oblige their government for the repeal of the separation of church and state and the reenactment of the medieval papacy in freedom-loving America.

The first beast—the medieval papacy—was a union of church and state. The image to the beast in America would be an American likeness to the medieval papacy—an American union of church and state. To accomplish this would mean the demolition of the constitutional protection of the separation of church and state. The false revival is what gives life to this movement that ushers in the union of church and state. Eventually the country is so permeated with this false revival that they appeal to the state to enforce their decrees and thus erect an image to the beast.

In the last decade we have witnessed the political arm of the charismatic movement develop into the "religious right." This "religious right" has attempted to influence the political process and has gained a respectable seat in the Republican party. Their stated aims seem innocent at first glance, but the eventual result is the imposition of their religious beliefs on the rest of the populace. That is precisely the road to be traveled by this false revival.

In the mid-70s, America first heard of the "religious right" in the election of Jimmy Carter. He was the first presidential candidate to appeal to the "religious right" as the "born again" president. Thereafter every serious presidential candidate has claimed to be born again. Suddenly, the "religious right" realized they had political clout and that the politicians would listen to their agenda. This platform expanded in the election of Ronald Reagan in 1980. Here was a candidate fully endorsed by the "religious right" and promising to help fulfill their agenda of returning America to religion. Much of their public agenda has been expressed in the appeal to return to "family values," but their hidden agenda of political control to enforce religious beliefs is inherently there. President Bush continued in 1988 to appeal to this group in his election bid. In 1992, the "religious right" supported Pat Buchanan in the primary season, because they claimed that George Bush had abandoned their agenda to enact religious legislation. In response George Bush moved his position back into line with the agenda of the religious right, for he knew he could not be elected without their support.

What is the agenda of the "religious right"? While not publicly stated often, it comes out periodically. In the midst of the 1980 election, the Moral Majority arose, led by Jerry Falwell. Note this official editorial:

> Separation of church and state is a dangerous concept. This is because the phrase "separation of church and state" is not found in the constitution and the misuse of the phrase leads to all sorts of trouble—such as trying to keep godly principles out of legislation.
>
> We should be accurate in our use of the language of the constitution and in the coming years it is crucial that we be able to accurately explain the true meaning intended by the phrase.
>
> Our constitution prohibits the establishment of religion and guarantees the free exercise thereof. The "establishment clause" means that the Baptists, Assemblies of God, Catholics, Lutherans, or Mormon church can never become the "official church" in America. The free exercise clause means that the government is powerless to be involved in the regulation of belief or church activities. It does not mean that our beliefs cannot be legislated or church attending people elected to office. A thorough understanding of our constitution is vital to our survival. Let's talk more like the constitution and less like a bumper sticker. Wipe the phrase separation of church and state out of your vocabulary.—Editorial, Moral Majority's Washington State Newspaper, August 1980.

In view of Revelation 13's prediction, this statement is absolutely astounding. Talking out of both sides of their mouth, Moral Majority claimed to support the constitution, but at the same time wished to eliminate the basic right and guarantee of the constitution—the separation of church and state. Note the avowed purpose of this constitutional repudiation: so that beliefs can be legislated.

Eventually, the Moral Majority was disbanded by Jerry Falwell, not because he repudiated its aims, but because others had taken up the mantle and his leadership was no longer needed there. Following the demise of the Moral Majority, Rev. Moon's Unification Church has picked up some of this mantle, uniting these different religious groups:

> Moon says, "Separation between religion and politics is what Satan likes most." But former Unification Church official Michael Warder says, "Within the Moon movement, there is no foundation for the ideas of freedom, the rule of law and the dignity of the individual as they are understood in the West."

> In the fall of 1986, as the Rev. Jerry Falwell's Moral Majority was in retreat, Pak and Jarmin met with several other conservatives to plan an explicitly Christian third party that, in the words of one participant, would attract religious people repelled by the "more atheistic and nonreligious Republican and Democratic parties."

> Because almost all conservative organizations in Washington have some ties to the church, conservatives also fear repercussions if they expose the church's role."—*US News and World Report*, March 27, 1989.

Another part of the mantle fell on Pat Robertson, whose unsuccessful bid for the Republican nomination in 1988 has not kept him out of the political arena. Robertson makes no bones about his stated aim to restore America to God through the political process. While many Christians share Robertson's concern that there is a tremendous need for people in America to come to Christ and to return to religious values, many are frightened by his attempt to accomplish this through the political process, especially in view of the prediction of Revelation 13.

In his recent book, *The New World Order*, Pat Robertson clearly defines his political agenda. He has little respect for the constitution of the United States—especially the first amendment that guarantees the separation of church and state. In his book, he refers to the founding fathers before the constitution as the guiding light for America today:

> The founders of America—at Plymouth Rock and in the Massachusetts Colony—felt that they were organizing a society based on the Ten Commandments and the Sermon on the Mount. They perceived this new land as a successor to the nation of Israel, and they tried their best to model their institutions of governmental order after the Bible. In fact the man who interpreted the meaning of Scripture to them, the pastor, was given a higher place than the governor of the colony. These people built an incredible society because they exalted "the mountain of the Lord's house" above the other mountains.

> There is no other way to explain the success of this experiment in liberty other than to realize that for almost two hundred years prior to our Constitution, all of the leadership of this nation had been steeped in the biblical principles of the Old and New Testaments. Their new order was

a nation founded squarely on concepts of the nature of God, the nature of man, the role of the family, and the moral order as established by the God of Jacob.—Pat Robertson, *The New World Order*, p. 246.

Robertson states that he desires to return America to the kind of government that existed prior to the establishment of the constitution. What he fails to tell about that 200 years is that religious tyranny reigned in America, just as in Europe. The persecuted Pilgrims became the persecutors. That was the difference. People were required to attend church, keep the Sabbath (Sunday), and give offerings or face punishment. This was America before the constitution.

Who are to be the leaders in Robertson's new world order? On what basis will government be run? Listen to his startling words:

There will never be world peace until God's house and God's people are given their rightful place of leadership at the top of the world. How can there be peace when drunkards, drug dealers, communists, atheists, New Age worshipers of Satan, secular humanists, oppressive dictators, greedy moneychangers, revolutionary assassins, adulterers, and homosexuals are on top? Under their leadership the world will never, I repeat never, experience lasting peace . . .

Although I agree that it is unwise for the organized church as an institution to get itself entwined with government as an institution, there is absolutely no way that government can operate successfully unless led by godly men and women operating under the laws of the God of Jacob.—*Ibid.*, p. 227.

Robertson does not declare that it is wrong, but only unwise, for the church to get involved in politics at this time. In Robertson's view the only people who should lead this new world order are religious people who will enforce religious principles. Whose religion? His!

Robertson further declares that the only law that should govern society in his new world order is the Ten Commandments. It is true that the Ten Commandments are the basic law upon which society is built, but to enforce the religious obligations of the Ten Commandments creates religious totalitarianism.

> Without saying so explicitly, the Ten Commandments set the only order that will bring world peace—with devotion to and respect of God at the center, strong family bonds and respect next, and the sanctity of people, property, family, reputation, and peace of mind next.—*Ibid*, p. 233.

> The next obligation that a citizen of God's world order owes is to himself. "Remember the Sabbath day, to keep it holy," is a command for the personal benefit of each citizen. . . . Only when people are permitted to rest from their labors, to meditate on God, to consider His way, to dream of a better world can there be progress and genuine human betterment. . . . Laws in America that mandated a day of rest from incessant commerce have been nullified as a violation of the separation of church and state.—*Ibid*, p. 236.

In Robertson's new world order, the Ten Commandments are enforced, including his interpretation of the fourth, which he believes enjoins society to require people to keep Sunday. If one reads between the lines in the above statement, it appears that one of the reasons he laments the separation of church and state is because this concept has prevented them from enforcing Sunday observance. Of course, this was clearly prescribed in American society prior to the constitution, with dire penalties for Sabbath violation.

Robertson's aim is to take control of the United States in this decade. His well-thought-out plans are aimed at capturing American politics and setting in place his Christian agenda. While his goal is seemingly unrealistic at this time, yet it points to his ultimate objective—the control of the U.S. government:

> My goal is to see a pro-freedom majority in the United States Senate in 1992, and a reversal of leadership in the House of Representatives by 1996. My associates are now publishing a newspaper called the *Christian American,* which is slated for a circulation of 10 million during this decade.—*Ibid,* p. 261.

Many Christians would favor much of what Robertson talks about. The difference, however, is that Robertson wants to create his new world order by gaining control of government and forcing everyone to conform. God does not accept such worship. Service and obedience to God must spring forth spontaneously from love, not because of government obligation.

The fascinating thing is that both Pat Robertson and his Christian right and Pope John Paul II have identical aims—the control of the new world order. What will happen in the future is uncertain at the moment. How fast they can achieve their agenda is uncertain. But the direction of both groups is obvious and needs to be watched carefully in the light of the prediction of Revelation 13.

Under the Reagan and Bush administrations, the United States has inherited the legacy of an increasingly conservative Supreme Court that no longer values individual liberties with the same concern that the previous Supreme Court had guaranteed.

As a result of the explosive world developments of the last few years, several events have occurred that seem to be setting the world up for the final fulfillment of Bible prophecy in the new world order. Communism—the king of the south—has fallen. The papacy and America have emerged as the leaders. At the same time, the conservative element is attempting to gain control of American government, and movements are underfoot to eliminate the separation of church and state and enforce the religious beliefs of the religious right by governmental decree. America, in the aftermath of the Gulf War, has suddenly emerged as the undisputed world leader. All the world looks to her for leadership. For the first time in her history, America is poised to fulfill the prophetic role of Revelation 13. Meanwhile, the Pope waits for a supernatural sign that will bring America fully into his camp. America will then lead the world to the papal banner. Thus will be born the totally new world order reestablishing of preeminence of Rome in controlling the world. Revelation 13:15-17 describes the scene that follows the final establishment of the new world order:

And he had power to give life unto the image of

the beast, that the image of the beast should both speak, and cause that as many as would not worship the image of the beast should be killed. And he causeth all, both small and great, rich and poor, free and bond, to receive a mark in their right hand, or in their foreheads: And that no man might buy or sell, save he that had the mark, or the name of the beast, or the number of his name. (Revelation 13:15-17.)

Those who refuse to comply with this new world order will be killed. The death penalty will be reenacted for religious dissenters, just as it was when the papacy ruled the world in the Dark Ages. The mark of the first beast—the sign of allegiance to this papal power—will then be enforced by legislation, and no one will be able to buy or sell unless he recognizes the supremacy of the papal power as he governs the new world order.

This will be an extremely trying time for God's people, who refuse to acknowledge the new world order. With economic restrictions and the death penalty in place, it would appear not to be long until they are eliminated, unless God should intervene. God's people will be in the minority. If the new world order could conquer them, its dominion would be universal. That is why, with great fury, it attacks the people of God with economic restrictions and a death decree. The time has come for earth's final showdown— the battle of Armageddon. This is when the last king of the north—the new world order with the Pope in control—seeks to plant its tabernacle of control in the glorious holy mountain. But, thank God, He intervenes. The time of defeat for God's people turns into a triumphant conclusion to the great controversy, as Christ Himself leads the armies of heaven to stand for God's people in this trying hour.

9

Devilish Spirits and the New Age

Spiritualistic seances, reincarnation, psychic phenomena, and spirit communication are just a few of the many occult interests sweeping America at the end of the twentieth century. In fact, the New Age has emerged right alongside the new world order. According to Revelation 16:13, 14, two movements merge to create the image to the beast that we examined in the previous chapter.

Revelation 13 has predicted that the whole world will unite to oppose those loyal to Christ and will seek to destroy these true worshippers of God.

Scripture indicates increased spiritualistic psychic phenomena taking place on a global scale as the world approaches Armageddon.

> And I saw three unclean spirits like frogs come out of the mouth of the dragon, and out of the mouth of the beast, and out of the mouth of the false prophet. For they are the spirits of devils, working miracles, which go forth unto the kings of the earth and of the whole world, to gather them to the battle of that great day of God Almighty. (Revelation 16:13, 14.)

Along with the tongues and miraculous signs produced by the religious right (see chapter 8), Revelation 16 indicates there will be increased occult activity. In fact, it may well be that increased psychic phenomena pave the way for the false miracles and tongues that sweep the religious world. In both cases they are appealing to the miraculous as a source of truth. This makes it possible for the devil to take the whole world captive in his delusions.

Over the last several years we have witnessed a great increase in spirit activity in our world. From the simple ouija board in the living room of thousands of Americans to the sophisticated seances occurring in darkened chambers, people are seeking to find answers to the bewildering problems of modern living. Even people of renown in government have been known to seek psychic advice in order to find the answers to the unanswerable problems facing us at the end of the twentieth century.

Hollywood has been slowly and subtly conditioning our minds to the possibilities of the New

Age. Not only movies, but many television programs boldly present New Age and occult ideas as established facts. Hollywood's version of the afterlife is simply a place where one goes to get reassigned to a new body on this earth. Even in many "good" films, subtle New Age thinking is being presented. For example, angels are simply human beings who are sent back to earth after they die to try and help people. In this way, they finally earn their right to move on to heaven. Very slyly, salvation by works is being taught by many of these films—merely a modern version of the medieval purgatory.

Some of the most beloved and popular films of our day undermine basic Christianity with New Age thinking. The popular "Star Wars" films took the basic Bible story of the controversy between good and evil and relegated it to intergalactic space. Instead of "God be with you," people now said "the force be with you." Insidiously, the force had replaced God. Even one of the most popular films of all time, "E.T.," undermined basic Christianity by substituting E.T. for Christ. For example, in the closing scenes of the film, E.T. dies, is clothed in a white linen shroud, is resurrected, and ascends into the heavens as those who found him look on. Those scenes bear unmistakable references to the death, burial, resurrection, and ascension of Jesus. In the minds of many Americans, E.T. and the heroes of "Star Wars" have replaced Christ and the Christian heaven.

Interest in the occult and the extraterrestrial is mushrooming across America and the world today as Planet Earth prepares for the final onslaught of the spirits of devils.

> From Manhattan to Malibu, a big and bizarre
> business is springing up as Americans look for
> supernatural answers to real-life problems. Psy-
> chics are collecting up to $250 an hour for making
> predictions and "channeling" advice from enti-
> ties, alleged spirits from another world or an-
> other time. The number of professional channels
> in California alone tops 1000. One of them, Jack
> Pursel of San Francisco grosses more than $1
> million a year on seminars, counseling, and
> videocassetes as the medium for a spirit known
> as "Lazarus, the consummate friend."—US News
> and World Report, February 9, 1987.

A whole generation of people not educated in
basic biblical beliefs have now come upon the
American scene. They are desperately searching
for spiritual answers to the problems of life. The
New Age and the occult are providing that which,
in past generations, Christianity supplied.

According to Revelation 13 and 16, the New Age
movement will unite Protestants and Catholics in
the final great apostasy that will sweep across
Planet Earth in the closing hours of earth's history.
Miracles, signs, wonders, healings, and fire from
heaven are all supernatural events used to bring
about the image to the beast. (See the previous
chapter.) Yet there is another side to all of this. The
New Age movement, with its occult tendencies,
will blend with the tongues, miracles, and signs of
the religious right. Even the secular press has noticed this amazing connection, foretold in Revelation 13:

> Ministers generally dismiss the psychic boom as
> idolatry and false religion. Some religious lead-
> ers and other critics see the mystic view of man,

with its belief in an inner divinity and reincarnation, as leading to amorality, an indifference to
social responsibilities and a rejection of Judeo-
Christian values. Even so, there are signs that
conventional religious organizations are re-
sponding to the new interest. No mainstream
church endorses channeling, but Constant Jac-
quet, editor of the National Council of Churches'
yearbook of churches, reports a surge in faith
healing among Episcopalians. There's also a revival of Jewish mystic practices and meditation
training in Roman Catholic monasteries. "Never
underestimate the ability of organized religion to
adapt," says Harvard theologian Harvey Cox.
"It's very market conscious."—*US News and
World Report*, February 9, 1987, article: "Mystics
on Main Street," p. 69.

Amazingly, even the secular press sees a relationship between the New Age and the miraculous
things happening within the Christian Church.
There could very well be a real connection between
the devil's attempt to link the occult, with its New
Age philosophy, and Christianity, as he attempts
to bring about the final great deception of all time.

It should also be pointed out that much of what
is occurring in the New Age and occult movements
can be accounted for by misrepresentation and
fraud. Yet much of it is real. These things *are* happening. Unless a Christian is fortified with answers from God's Word, that person is apt to be
deceived by the New Age.

In this chapter we wish to examine closely the
New Age's claim to spirit communication and reincarnation. Neither of these very basic New Age
beliefs is really new. They stem from old polythe-
ism and paganism. Yet they have been marketed

in modern terms. Basic to the New Age is belief in the immortality of the soul and life immediately after death in another world where those who have arrived can still communicate with people in this world.

Christianity is unique among world religions. It is the only religion that preaches the doctrine of the literal bodily resurrection. To the pagans, life after death meant a spirit existence. However, Christianity, like Judaism before it, never taught the doctrine of the immortality of the soul. The doctrine of the resurrection, taught embryonically in Judaism, is fully developed in New Testament Christianity. Here it is presented as the foundational doctrine of the Christian faith. Note the stirring words of the apostle Paul on the essentials of the doctrine of the resurrection:

> But if there be no resurrection of the dead, then is Christ not risen: And if Christ be not risen, then is our preaching vain, and your faith is also vain. And if Christ be not raised, your faith is vain; ye are yet in your sins. Then they also which are fallen asleep in Christ are perished. (1 Corinthians 15:13, 14, 17, 18.)

Paul's point is crystal clear. If there is no resurrection, then those who have died are perished. They have no hope of life after death except through the resurrection. Yet, if one went to heaven at death, one would have life after death without resurrection. The safest course against New Age thinking is the biblical concept of the resurrection hope.

Another clear early doctrine of Christianity was the hope of the second coming of Christ. Jesus

Himself declared that the purpose of His return would be to take His faithful people to heaven.

> In my Father's house are many mansions: if it were not so, I would have told you. I go to prepare a place for you. And if I go and prepare a place for you, I will come again, and receive you unto myself; that where I am, there ye may be also. (John 14:2, 3.)

If people went to heaven at death, there would be no need for Christ to return to take them to the Father's house. Why should He come to take them where they already are? No wonder that when the doctrine of the immortal soul entered the Christian church in the third century, the church stopped emphasizing the resurrection and second coming of Jesus.

The Bible also declares that humans are mortal—subject to death. Immortality is something that is not received until the second coming of Jesus.

> Behold, I shew you a mystery; We shall not all sleep, but we shall all be changed, In a moment, in the twinkling of an eye, at the last trump: for the trumpet shall sound, and the dead shall be raised incorruptible, and we shall be changed. For this corruptible must put on incorruption, and this mortal must put on immortality. (1 Corinthians 15:51-53.)

If immortality is something received at the second coming, then no one possesses it now. Yet the New Age pictures everyone with an immortal soul. Again, if a person already possessed it, why would he need it at the second coming of Christ? In fact, the Bible is so dogmatic on this point that it even declares that immortality is an attribute of

Deity and that God is the sole possessor of immortality:

> Now unto the King eternal, immortal, invisible, the only wise God, be honour and glory for ever and ever. Amen. (1 Timothy 1:17.)

> Which in his times he shall shew, who is the blessed and only Potentate, the King of kings, and Lord of lords; Who only hath immortality. (1 Timothy 6:15, 16.)

Amazingly, New Age believers and even many Christians have been bewitched by the devil into accepting the pagan notion of an immortal soul, in spite of the fact that the Bible clearly declares God to be the sole possessor of immortality. For man to claim that which is uniquely God's is blasphemy.

Immortality means to be incapable of dying. The glorious promise of the gospel of Christ is that God will bestow immortality on the saints at the second coming of Jesus (1 Corinthians 15:51-53). It is the great promise of John 3:16:

> For God so loved the world, that he gave his only begotten Son, that whosoever believeth in him should not perish, but have everlasting life.

This is the very reason God has given us His Son—so that we might possess immortality, or eternal life. However, if human beings already possess it, why did Jesus have to die on the cross? To give us that which was innately ours to begin with, as the New Age teaches?

Note how Satan has insidiously destroyed the Christian faith through the New Age movement and its belief in the immortal soul. If a person possesses an immortal soul, there is no need for the resurrection, no need for the second coming, and no need for the cross of Christ. With one sweeping stroke, Satan has destroyed the very foundation of Christianity.

Even secular writers recognize the pagan origin of the belief in the immortality of the soul or life immediately after death.

> And Hughes argues that the traditional belief in unending punishment is linked to the erroneous belief in the "innate immortality" of the soul — a belief, he says, that is based more on Plato than on the Bible. — *US News and World Report*, March 25, 1991, p. 63. Article: "Hell's Sober Comeback."

One must be acutely aware not only of the origin of the doctrine of the immortal soul in Greek mythology — as popularized by Plato — but also that this ancient Greek mythology is once again contending for the attention of millions of people today through the New Age movement.

If people are mortal, then, and do not have life after death until the resurrection, what happens to them in the interval between death and resurrection? Only the Bible can accurately answer that question.

> For the living know that they shall die; but the dead know not any thing, neither have they any more a reward; for the memory of them is forgotten. Also their love, and their hatred, and their envy, is now perished; neither have they any more a portion for ever in any thing that is done under the sun. (Ecclesiastes 9:5, 6.)

> Put not your trust in princes, nor in the son of man, in whom there is no help. His breath goeth forth, he returneth to his earth; in that very day his thoughts perish. (Psalm 146:3, 4.)

> No one remembers you when he is dead. Who praises you from the grave? (Psalm 6:5, NIV.)

> Men and brethren, let me speak freely to you of the patriarch David, that he is both dead and buried, and his tomb is with us to this day . . . For David did not ascend into the heavens. (Acts 2:28, 34, NKJV.)

The Scriptures are explicit. Spirit communication is an impossibility, because the dead no longer have anything to do with anything done under the sun. When people die, they know nothing, they have no thoughts, they don't praise God or even remember God. That is certainly hard to imagine if in fact they were enjoying the bliss of heaven. According to Peter, the mighty David—a man after God's own heart—was still in the tomb a thousand years after he died.

When Jesus was faced with the death of his friend Lazarus, He declared that Lazarus was asleep (John 11:11-14). He came to bring comfort and hope to Mary and Martha, Lazarus' sisters. Note that the hope Jesus brought was the Christian hope of resurrection, not the pagan notion of an immortal soul in heaven.

> Jesus said unto her, I am the resurrection, and the life: he that believeth in me, though he were dead, yet shall he live. (John 11:25.)

The only hope Jesus can give is resurrection hope. And Jesus grants it immediately by calling Lazarus forth from the tomb, not down from heaven. The word Jesus used to describe death, "sleep," is used over 100 times in the Scriptures to denote death. Again, the apostle Paul reiterates this hope to the Thessalonians who were losing loved ones:

> For the Lord himself shall descend from heaven
> with a shout, with the voice of the archangel, and
> with the trump of God: and the dead in Christ
> shall rise first: Then we which are alive and re-
> main shall be caught up together with them in
> the clouds to meet the Lord in the air: and so shall
> we ever be with the Lord. Wherefore comfort one
> another with these words. (1 Thessalonians 4:16-
> 18.)

This is the hope of Christianity. Satan wishes to
rob us of this unique hope by substituting the
pagan notion of the immortal soul. How much
better is the biblical hope of the resurrection, where
we will be real people with real physical bodies
doing real things! Don't let Satan deceive you on
this foundational doctrine of Christianity.

So what about the New Age teaching of spiritualistic communication and the doctrine of reincarnation? Absolutely impossible, if we
believe the Bible. Our best answer to the New
Age is the biblical teaching that the dead do not
know anything. They are asleep and cannot communicate with the living.

Who then are these so-called "spirits" of spiritualistic phenomena? The Bible rightly describes
them as the spirits of devils masquerading as dead
people (Revelation 16:14). They may claim supe-
rior knowledge and divine insights, but Christians
must remember they come from the prince of dark-
ness. It is impossible for the dead to communicate
through any medium, because Scripture declares
the dead know nothing. Nor is reincarnation a
possibility. If there is no immortal soul separate
from the body, then it is impossible for a soul to
inhabit another body and live another life. Make

no mistake about it. There is only one life we get to live. The decisions we make here will determine our eternal destiny.

Soon the New Age movement will unite with the signs, wonders, and tongues of the false revival. This combination will join with Protestants and Catholics for the final great union of Babylon the Great. Satan will then seek in the Battle of Armageddon to wipe from the face of Planet Earth those who will not accept his New Age and his new world order. Let's examine earth's final battle in the next chapter.

10

Showdown of the Ages

I t's time for the showdown! For over 6,000 years, God has allowed Satan to attack and conquer His people. Now the time has come for Michael to stand up and deliver His people in the ultimate battle of the universe. The stage is now set. The players are in place. The event is ready to begin. Earth's final battle is approaching.

Several prophetic scriptures describe this fearful battle. We have examined them closely throughout this book. Let's put them together now as we reach the climax of history.

> And at the time of the end shall the king of the south push at him: and the king of the north shall come against him like a whirlwind, with chariots, and with horsemen, and with many ships;

and he shall enter into the countries, and shall overflow and pass over. He shall stretch forth his hand also upon the countries: and the land of Egypt shall not escape. But he shall have power over the treasures of gold and of silver, and over all the precious things of Egypt; and the Libyans and the Ethiopians shall be at his steps. But tidings out of the east and out of the north shall trouble him: therefore he shall go forth with great fury to destroy, and utterly to make away many. And he shall plant the tabernacles of his palace between the seas in the glorious holy mountain; yet he shall come to his end, and none shall help him.

And at that time shall Michael stand up, the great prince which standeth for the children of thy people: and there shall be a time of trouble, such as never was since there was a nation even to that same time: and at that time thy people shall be delivered, every one that shall be found written in the book. (Daniel 11:40-12:1.)

And the dragon was wroth with the woman, and went to make war with the remnant of her seed, which keep the commandments of God, and have the testimony of Jesus Christ. (Revelation 12:17.) And deceiveth them that dwell on the earth by the means of those miracles which he had power to do in the sight of the beast; saying to them that dwell on the earth, that they should make an image to the beast, which had the wound by a sword, and did live. And he had power to give life unto the image of the beast, that the image of the beast should both speak, and cause that as many as would not worship the image of the beast should be killed. And he causeth all, both small and great, rich and poor, free and bond, to receive a mark in their right hand, or in their foreheads: And that no man might buy or sell save he that had the mark, or the name of the beast, or the number of his name. (Revelation 13:14-17.)

And the sixth angel poured out his vial upon the great river Euphrates; and the water thereof was dried up, that the way of the kings of the east might be prepared. And I saw three unclean spirits like frogs come out of the mouth of the dragon, and out of the mouth of the beast, and out of the mouth of the false prophet. For they are the spirits of devils, working miracles, which go forth unto the kings of the earth and of the whole world, to gather them to the battle of that great day of God Amighty. Behold, I come as a thief. Blessed is he that watcheth, and keepeth his garments, lest he walk naked, and they see his shame. And he gathered them together into a place called in the Hebrew tongue Armageddon. And the seventh angel poured out his vial into the air; and there came a great voice out of the temple of heaven, from the throne, saying, It is done. And there were voices, and thunders, and lightnings; and there was a great earthquake, such as was not since men were upon the earth, so mighty an earthquake, and so great. (Revelation 16:12-18.)

All four of these passages are describing the same event—the final climactic battle of earth between the forces of good and the forces of evil—the final battle of the great controversy. This battle seeks the total annihilation of the people of God from Planet Earth, but consummates in total victory for the saints of God. Jesus Christ Himself intervenes in this conflict to deliver the victorious ones.

This final battle is precipitated by the United

States taking the lead in bringing the world under the umbrella of Rome. While America may continue her political power, she will be subservient to the power of Rome. She will rule with Rome's permission, just as kings reigned in the Dark Ages. All the world will follow America's example and acknowledge the supremacy of Rome.

In fact, only a small group of people will refuse to bow in obeisance to the power of Rome. This will anger the beast, and he will determine to blot out of existence those who resist his rule. Rome sought to destroy the keepers of the faith in the Dark Ages; in the final conflict, similar scenes will be repeated. The earthquakes, wars, economic problems, drug crimes, et cetera have brought the world to the place where the only answer seems to be religious control of the people. That's why the world so willingly falls into the camp of Rome again. Those who fail to comply are labeled as communists, drug dealers, or worse. But whatever they are called, the only desire of Rome is to rid the earth of those who resist her ways. Then and only then can her rulership be complete.

These who resist—the saints of Revelation 12:17 who keep the commandments of God and have the testimony of Jesus—make Satan angry. If only he could eliminate them, none would then oppose him. Thus the focus of the last battle is this remnant people who do not acknowledge the supremacy of Rome. This is a very real, literal battle, but it is not a military conflict between competing nations. Rather it is a real physical battle fought over spiritual issues. This is earth's real Armageddon.

The Battle of Armageddon

As the earth moves forward toward the end, all the powers of evil unite in their attempt to destroy God's remnant. This brings the world to the final battle—the Battle of Armageddon. All seems to be going in favor of spiritual Babylon (Rome). Then suddenly, Scripture declares, the River Euphrates is dried up (Revelation 16:12). This infuriates spiritual Babylon and forces her to launch her final attack.

The River Euphrates wound through the ancient city of Babylon, which was built by Nebuchadnezzar. The river provided support to the city, giving it a constant water supply. Ingeniously, Cyrus, the Persian whom God had raised up to deliver His people from Babylonian captivity, devised a method to enter the city. He had his men dig an alternate channel. Then one evening, while the Babylonians were in a drunken party, Cyrus diverted the river and marched his troops through the river bed, under the city walls, and through the flood gate that the drunken Babylonians had left open. That night ancient Babylon became history.

Revelation 16:12 declares that the Euphrates will once again be dried up to prepare the way for the kings of the east. Scripture named Cyrus as the righteous man from the east (Isaiah 41:2-4) when he came to deliver God's people. To accomplish that deliverance, God dried up the Euphrates to prepare the way for the kings of the east—Cyrus and his forces. Likewise, Revelation 16 depicts spiritual Babylon now sitting on the pinnacle of success, with the whole world—except for the remnant—at her fingertips. Then Babylon's support is suddenly withdrawn. Those powers that have supported her turn away—her Euphrates dries up. This drying up occurs to prepare the way for the ultimate Deliverer of God's people—Jesus Christ—who is about to come as King of kings and Lord of lords. He is the final King of the East.

The outpouring of the seven vials will have infuriated the three powers controlling Babylon. The world was supposed to get better under her leadership. That's why all the nations had entered her camp. She had convinced them that God, working through Rome, was the only solution to the world's great problems, but the outpouring of the vials shows that conditions are only getting worse. Babylon senses that her support, the Euphrates, is drying up. This angers her. In great fury she quickly gathers her forces to destroy the remnant (Revelation 16:14, 15; Daniel 11:44, 45). In so doing, she is preparing for war against the God of heaven; She has entered the battle of the great day of God Almighty.

As the remnant see the forces being gathered to wipe them out of existence, they realize that the end is near. The place of this final conflict is called Armageddon (Revelation 16:16). What is the meaning of Armageddon?

The word *Armageddon* appears only one time in the Bible, in Revelation 16:16. Here we are told that it is called Armageddon in the Hebrew tongue. Hebrew is the language of the Old Testament. Therefore, to understand the Battle of Armageddon, one must look into the Old Testament. No place on earth is now, or has ever been, called Armageddon. Therefore, we must look for a symbolic meaning of the name.

Armageddon comes from two Hebrew words. The first is *har*, meaning "mountain" or "hill." The etymology of the second part of the word is debated by scholars. Some have suggested it comes from the Hebrew "maggeddon," meaning "Megiddo." Megiddo referred to an ancient city in Old Testament times. There was also a plain of Megiddo where a famous battle of the Old Testament took place. Those who have accepted this interpretation have usually interpreted Armageddon as a literal battle occurring on the plain of Megiddo in the Middle East. The problem is that the word *Armageddon* would mean "hill of Megiddo" or "mountain of Megiddo." While there is a plain, a valley, and a city of Megiddo, there is no mountain of Megiddo located in the Middle East.

The other possibility is that the second part of the word comes from the Hebrew word *mo'ed*, which means "congregation" or "assembly." Thus, the basic meaning of Armageddon would be the "mount of the assembly," which in ancient Israel was Mount Zion—the symbol of the people of God. *Harmo'ed* is found one time in the Old Testament:

> For thou hast said in thine heart, I will ascend into heaven, I will exalt my throne above the stars of God: I will sit also upon the mount of the congregation, in the sides of the north. (Isaiah 14:13.)

This passage refers to Lucifer's original attempt to sit where God sat. Lucifer wished to have control of the glorious holy mountain. Now, at the end of the great controversy, we see that Satan has not changed. He still wishes to control Mount Zion, the church of the living God. In this setting Armageddon would refer to Satan's final attempt to destroy the remnant church of Christ and place his throne of control over God's people.

Here appears the same basic word as found in Revelation 16:16. Since Revelation 16:16 indicates that it is to be found in the Hebrew tongue, and since this is the only place it is found in the Old Testament, we can only assume that this is the correct interpretation of the word. This is made evident when we also discover that only this interpretation completely meshes with the entire scenario of last-day events as they are outlined in the rest of Daniel and Revelation. There is also a strong tie in Armageddon to Daniel 11:45, where the final king of the north attempts to place his tabernacle in the beautiful holy mountain. This is obviously the same event as the battle of Armageddon predicted in Revelation 16.

What causes spiritual Babylon—the final king of the north—to move with such quick fury against the remnant of Revelation 12:17? Clearly, something has happened that lets this power know that its time is short. Daniel 11:44 gives us a hint: "tidings out of the east and the north trouble him." Why? The true king of the north is about to speak and reassert Himself as the rightful ruler of the world. This makes the usurper violent. In addition, tidings out of the east disturb him, because he sees the signs of the approaching Son of Man to deliver God's people. Scripture declares that Christ will come as lightning shining from the east to the west (Matthew 24:27). East seems to be the point of the compass assigned in Scripture for the coming of Christ. Remember that the Euphrates in Revelation 16:12 is dried up to prepare the way for the kings of the East. Christ is the King of the East, and comes as King of kings.

Thus, the Battle of Armageddon is not a battle fought in the Middle East. It is not a political war over oil fields. It is a religious battle fought by a combined religio-political power of the last days that attempts to destroy the remnant people of God, who keep the commandments of God and have the testimony of Jesus Christ.

The Battle Begins

Infuriated by a turn of events that seems out of his control, the final king of the north (mighty spiritual Babylon—the American-Roman union) suddenly realizes that time is running out. Satan leads them to believe that if they could somehow snuff out the people of God, they could prevent the end of the world and usher in the long awaited millennium of peace.

Perhaps a council is held and a decision is made that in one night they will completely destroy the saints of God. They have already imposed economic sanctions against God's people, for no one can buy or sell unless they show allegiance to this power (Revelation 13:16, 17). That has not worked; God's people have remained faithful. They will not yield. Finally, a new tactic is proposed—to wipe the saints from the face of the earth—a death decree for all who oppose the grand union (Revelation 13:15).

As these apostate forces gather around the remnant, preparing in one night to destroy them from the face of the earth, God stands ready to interfere and deliver His chosen ones as verily as He did the three Hebrews in the fiery furnace in ancient Babylon. Mighty Babylon has filled her cup of iniquity. Her time has run out. God will ring down the curtain and win the final battle by delivering His people who have stood firm for Him in the most trying circumstances the world has ever witnessed.

As the throngs of evil men are about to rush upon their prey, one can imagine that a cloud of dense blackness falls on the earth. Suddenly a rainbow, shining from the throne of God, seems to encircle each praying company. The righteous have not accumulated weapons of war. Their only weapon has been their spiritual relationship with God, which He now honors. As the wicked gaze upon the righteous, they are stopped in their tracks, their murderous rage suddenly forgotten. All they desire is to be shielded from the brightness of the light of God.

The people of God hear a voice saying, "Look up." They see the Son of God sitting on the throne, and from His lips they hear the request of John 17:24:

> Father, I will that they also, whom thou hast given me, be with me where I am: that they may behold my glory, which thou hast given me: for thou lovedst me before the foundation of the world.

God interposes and ends the great controversy by delivering His remnant, who are faithful to Him. This occurs under the seventh plague of Revelation 16:17-21:

And the seventh angel poured out his vial into the air; and there came a great voice out of the temple of heaven, from the throne, saying, It is done. And there were voices, and thunders, and lightnings; and there was a great earthquake, such as was not since men were upon the earth, so mighty an earthquake, and so great. And the great city was divided into three parts, and the cities of the nations fell: and great Babylon came in remembrance before God, to give unto her the cup of the wine of the fierceness of his wrath. And every island fled away, and the mountains were not found. And there fell upon men a great hail out of heaven, every stone about the weight of a talent: and men blasphemed God because of the plague of the hail; for the plague thereof was exceeding great.

A voice from heaven cries, "It is done!" There are voices, earthquakes, thunderings, and lightning. Everything in nature seems to be out of course; every mountain and island is moved out of its place (Revelation 6:14).

The whole earth heaves and swells like the waves of the sea. Its surface is breaking up. Its very foundations seem to be giving way. Mountain chains are sinking. Inhabited islands disappear. The seaports that have become like Sodom for wickedness are swallowed up by the angry waters.—E.G. White, *The Great Controversy*, p. 637.

Mighty hailstones begin falling, each weighing nearly a hundred pounds. The proud cities of earth are laid low. Prison walls fall away, and God's people—those imprisoned during the economic sanctions imposed under the mark of the beast—are set free. Babylon completely falls into the three parts that united it: Romanism, apostate American Protestantism, and spiritualism.

The people of God look up and see Jesus coming in the clouds of heaven. They watch the cloud of angels carrying the Saviour as He draws nearer and nearer to the earth (Revelation 19:11, 14). The sky seems filled with radiant forms—ten thousand times ten thousand. No human pen can adequately portray the scene, no mortal mind is adequate to conceive its splendor, as Jesus Christ returns to earth as King of kings and Lord of lords (Revelation 19:16).

The wicked cannot bear to look upon the splendor of the returning Christ. The terror of eternal despair falls upon them. All faces gather paleness (Jeremiah 30:6). Perhaps even the righteous call out as they view the magnitude of the scene transpiring before them: "Who shall be able to stand?" Very quickly the reassuring voice of Jesus is heard: "My grace is sufficient for you." Their faces light up, and joy fills every heart as they realize their deliverance is at hand.

Then all the faces of the wicked gather paleness as they see the Saviour they have spurned. There is silence, and nothing is heard but the voice of prayer. It will be the greatest prayer meeting ever held in the history of this world—a prayer meeting attended by every living soul. Lips that have never uttered a prayer will speak then. Those who rarely pray now will pray then, not because they want to, but because they are compelled to. They will not pray to God, but to the rocks and mountains to fall on them (Revelation 6:15-17).

As the wicked hear the voice of God, they recognize it as the voice that so often pleaded with them to repent, but to which they refused to listen. It awakens memories which they would fain blot out—of warnings despised, invitations refused, privileges slighted.

Suddenly, the voice of Christ is heard calling forth the sleeping saints: "Awake, Awake, ye that sleep in the dust of the earth, and arise." What a scene, as graves split wide open and the righteous dead spring forth to new life! Quickly, they unite their voices in one long, glad shout of victory (1 Corinthians 15:55). All blemishes and deformities are left in the grave. The living righteous are then changed and caught up in the air with the risen saints to meet their Lord. Little children are borne by the angels to their mother's arms. Friends separated by death are united. Together they ascend to the city of God.

This is the Battle of Armageddon! It appears at first that God's people have lost this battle, but as Daniel 12:1 indicates, it is at this time that Michael stands up for His people. It is a time of great trouble, but also a mighty time of victory for the people of God. Every one of His people ought to be longing for this glorious day, this blessed hope, when Armageddon arrives and God delivers His faithful saints.

As the righteous ascend to the city of God, they have the joy of being in the presence of their Redeemer—the One who delivered them so mightily. They behold the joy of Christ in seeing those saved by His death and humiliation. They fellowship again with loved ones with whom they have been reunited. But an even greater thrill is theirs as they see people with whom they had personally shared Jesus, now saved in the kingdom of God.

Now the two Adams are about to meet. In imagination we behold the Son of God standing with outstretched arms to receive the father of our race—the one whose sin caused the marks in His hands and feet.

As Adam discerns the prints of the cruel nails, he doesn't fall into Christ's bosom, but in humiliation at His feet, crying: "Worthy, worthy is the Lamb that was slain!" Tenderly, Christ lifts him up and bids him look again upon his Eden home, from which he has so long been exiled. Adam is now reinstated in his former dominion. And then in one grand chorus, all the redeemed bow at the feet of Jesus and take up the refrain: "Worthy, worthy is the Lamb that was slain!" (Revelation 7:10, 12).

What a day that will be—that day of deliverance for God's people at Armageddon, when Christ steps in to redeem His saints! That day is coming, and very soon. Are you ready to stand with God's remnant on the day of deliverance at Armageddon?

If you could know that Jesus would appear
  Before another morn should give its light,
Oh, would your heart be filled with joy or fear,
  If you could know that He would come tonight?
The things you'd do, the words that you would say,
Perhaps the letter that you'd thought to write,—
  How many plans would have to change today
If you were sure that Christ would come tonight?
  How many acts would then remain undone?
How many wrongs would have to be made right

If you should meet Him ere another sun,
And know for sure that He would come tonight?
How many things would you find room for then,
Now crowded out or else forgotten quite;
The kindly deed, the hour of prayer again—
Would aught be different should He come
tonight?
—Author Unknown

An anguished mother, bending over her dying child, was trying to soothe her by telling her about heaven. She spoke of the glory there, of the brightness reflected from the burnished streets, of the shining countenance of the holy angels. But presently a weak voice interrupted her, saying, "I don't think I would like that, Mama, because the light hurts my eyes."

Then the sad mother changed the angle of her description and spoke instead of the melodies above, of the harpers harping on their golden harps, of the voices like the sound of many waters, of the new song that they sing before the throne; but the little child said: "Mama, I just cannot bear any noise."

Grieved and disappointed at her failure to speak adequate words of comfort, the mother took the wasted little form from her restless bed and folded her close in the tenderness of her motherly arms. As the little sufferer lay there, she looked up into the face above her and whispered, "Mama, will YOU be there?"

How about it, dear reader, will YOU be there?

(The author acknowledges his indebtedness to the book, The Great Controversy *for much of the description found in this chapter.)*

11

Getting Ready for Glory

Walking down the streets of gold, fellowshipping for all eternity with loved ones and friends, searching into the very mind of God—these are just a few of the exciting adventures that await God's people in the kingdom to come. Yet the greatest joy of all will be that of being in the presence of our Saviour. What would you give for the privilege of spending eternity with Jesus?

Many people, even Christians, are afraid of last-day events and look forward to them with great foreboding. That need not be. The great day of God is to be a time of deliverance for God's people; it is a time to rejoice, not weep. The Bible refers to this event as the "blessed hope" (Titus 2:13). The world, as we have seen, may be in convulsion just before that great event, but the Christian is at peace during this time because of his relationship with his God. The most important thing each of us can do as we prepare for the climactic events of history, unfolding before our very eyes, is to develop a deep, abiding relationship with Jesus Christ.

Jesus Is My Lord

Last-day events are indeed frightening without Jesus as our Lord. There are people who need to fear the second coming of Christ; for they do not have a relationship with Him. They will call for the rocks and mountains to fall on them and hide them from the face of Jesus (Revelation 6:16, 17). Yet true Christians look up in peace, beholding the signs of Christ's coming, knowing that their day of deliverance is at hand. There is no fear, for perfect love has cast out fear (1 John 4:18).

Reader, do you desire the peace that only Jesus Christ can bring? Then you need to make certain that He is the Lord of your life. If you have not accepted Him as your own personal Saviour, I would like to invite you to do so now. There is no preparation for Christ's return as important as receiving Christ as Saviour and Lord. Jesus will not only accept you, regardless of your past, He will also forgive you of your sins, create in you a clean heart, and restore you completely to divine favor.

There are four simple steps that you need to take to receive Christ as your Lord and Saviour. If you have never taken them, you are invited to do so now.

Step 1. Believe that God loves you. Perhaps you have wondered if anyone could ever love you.

Maybe you have been put down all your life. No one seemed to care. Friend, Jesus cares, and He loves you. He proved His love for you beyond any shadow of doubt when He died on Calvary's cross. John 3:16 declares that "God so loved the world He gave His only begotten Son." God loved us while we were yet sinners, alienated from Him with no hope. If you have been tempted to doubt the love of God, then look to the cross. Jesus didn't have to go there; He went there only because of His great love for you. If you had been the only one in all of human history who would ever respond to that love, He would have gone to the cross just for you. That's how great the love of God is.

Step 2. Let the Holy Spirit lead you to repentance. Repentance is to turn away from sin in sorrow. Most of us are sorry when we get caught. That is not repentance. Repentance is to feel sorry because that sin sent Jesus to the cross. Real repentance comes when we realize what our sin cost the infinite God of the universe. Human ingenuity is incapable of producing this kind of repentance. It can come only as a gift from God (Acts 5:31). The second step is simply being willing to allow the Holy Spirit to bring us godly repentance and to turn us away from those sins from which God wishes to deliver us.

Step 3. Confess your sins. As the Holy Spirit leads us to repent of our sins, the response of our human heart must be the confession of the sins that the Holy Spirit convicts us of. Sins between God and us must be confessed directly to God and not to any other human being. And the promise of God is that if we confess, He will forgive our sins (1 John

1:9). Not only does Christ forgive us, but He also fully restores us, cleansing us of all unrighteousness. As a result we stand before God just as if we had never sinned.

Step 4. Invite Jesus into your life. Actually, this is the basic step that causes the other three to happen in our life. There comes that moment when each of us must decide for Christ. He will not force Himself upon us, but He offers to enter our lives, upon our invitation. All Jesus does is stand outside the door of our lives and knock (Revelation 3:20). We must open the door and invite Him in. When we do so, He promises that He will come in and fellowship with us. For the greatest experience of your life, just bow your head right now and give Him that special invitation to enter your life. You'll never regret this decision. Just pray this simple prayer:

> Lord Jesus, I am a sinner. I have failed You so often, but You have never failed me. I invite You to come into my life right now, forgive my sins, and give me new life and peace in Christ. Thank You for coming in. Amen.

What a joy! What a delight! You have been redeemed, born again, raised from spiritual death to spiritual life. You are now a new person in Christ Jesus. He is the new Lord of your life. You may be thinking: "But I didn't feel anything when I prayed." Some of us, because of our emotional make-up, feel more than others. However, Christ's entering our lives is not based on feeling, but on faith in His promise to enter our lives when we invite Him. You have asked Him into your life. Believe that He came in, not because you feel it, but because He has promised. Jesus says:

> Therefore I say to you, whatever things you ask when you pray, believe that you receive them, and you will have them. (Mark 11:24, NKJV.)

Do you believe, dear reader? If you do, then it has happened. Don't doubt, but rejoice in the accomplished fact. Jesus is your Lord. You are born again. You are a child of God. You are ready for Jesus to come. Note these reassuring words from John, the apostle who was closest to Jesus:

> And this is the record, that God hath given to us eternal life, and this life is in his Son. He that hath the Son hath life; and he that hath not the Son of God hath not life. These things have I written unto you that believe on the name of the Son of God; that ye may know that ye have eternal life, and that ye may believe on the name of the Son of God. (1 John 5:11-13.)

What assurance! We need not go through our spiritual life wondering about our relationship with God. We can have the assurance that when Jesus enters into our life, eternal life is ours NOW. That's why the Christian has peace as the world turns sour. His hope and faith are in the person of Jesus Christ who now is in control of his life. He is so anxious to meet this wonderful person called Jesus that he can't wait for the advent of his Lord. That's why it is called the blessed hope. Our Saviour and Redeemer is about to appear. O glorious day! That hope and peace is now yours in Christ.

A Relationship with Jesus

Having received Jesus Christ as your personal Saviour and Lord, it is now important that you develop a deep and abiding relationship with

Him. Everyone who has received Christ wants to get better acquainted with Him. Yet the good news is that Jesus also wants to get better acquainted with you. You see, that's how wonderful God is. He not only desires you to come to Him, but He wants to come to you. He not only wants you to learn about Him, but He wants to learn about you. He is the God of relationships.

Developing a relationship with Jesus is done in the same way as developing a deep relationship with a human being. It means taking time together, listening to your friend, talking together. As a Christian desiring a deeper relationship with Jesus, you will need to allow sufficient time to spend with your new Friend.

Basic to all relationships is listening. It is difficult to form a deep relationship with someone who is always talking. God speaks to us through His Word, the Holy Scriptures. That's why Christians need to set aside time each day for the study of God's Word. Develop a study program of your own, not just to get knowledge, but rather to learn more about your friend. Don't study just to discover a text that you can use to prove a point to someone, but instead always ask the question: What is God saying to me in this passage? Listen for the voice of God. Don't just read—listen as you read. Hear His voice. When you begin reading the Bible, start with the gospel of Mark or John. Get better acquainted with Jesus' life on earth. Then read the exciting story of the beginning of Christianity in the book of Acts, and move on to the writings of John and Paul. Read and reread as you ask God to open Himself to you.

The second ingredient of a relationship is communication. Not only do we need to study the Word and listen as the voice of God speaks to us, we must also talk to God. Remember that God doesn't simply want you to learn about Him; He also wants to learn about you. What a wonderful God! He has invited us to come into His very presence and talk with Him. We can have conversation with God! Sometimes people are afraid to pray for fear they don't have the right language. True prayer, however is not formal words, but a message directly from the heart. It is speaking to God as we would to any other person with whom we have an ongoing relationship. It is confiding to God all that troubles us and telling Him what we think of Him and what He means to us. Prayer is direct communication with the infinite God of the universe.

The third ingredient necessary to form a relationship is to spend time with that person. To have adequate communion with God, we will need to set aside time every day for Bible study, prayer, and meditation. Some people find that their relationship grows as they spend a half hour each day with God; others feel they need to spend at least an hour a day. In our busy schedules today, it is easy to skip this special time with God. Yet if we do not take this time, our relationship will soon begin to slip, just as any human relationship cools if we fail to spend adequate time together. Since this is the most important relationship in our lives, we must insure that adequate time is allocated each day for building our relationship with God.

A Special Day for
Building the Relationship

While a half hour or more each day is essential to

build our relationship with God, He indicates that we also need to devote one day each week exclusively to Him. In marital relationships, daily time with one's spouse is important, but it is also essential that a couple take a day each week and spend it together. If they do that, their relationship will grow much deeper than it otherwise would. God indicates that the same provision is essential for the divine relationship; each individual needs to spend one special day each week with God.

In the beginning of human history, before sin entered this world, God set aside a specific day which would be dedicated exclusively to fellowship between God and the men and women He had created. Notice the record of the day after God created Adam and Eve:

> And on the seventh day God ended his work which he had made; and he rested on the seventh day from all his work which he had made. And God blessed the seventh day, and sanctified it: because that in it he had rested from all his work which God created and made. (Genesis 2:2, 3.)

God had spent six days creating the vast world that Adam and Eve now inhabited. In the cool of that Friday evening, God came down to Adam and Eve and introduced them to the Sabbath—the memorial of all His creative activity. God did not give Adam and Eve the Sabbath because they needed to rest; they hadn't even worked yet. Nor did God give the Sabbath because He needed to rest; He is God. God gave the Sabbath at this critical time in Eden so that the humans whom He had created could spend this time with Him, celebrating what He had done. In this way God and man could become better acquainted and get to really know each other. Note that God's purpose in giving the Sabbath was not for rest, but for the development of a deep and abiding relationship between God and mankind. Our God is a God of relationships. He really wants to know us. So He has set aside one day each week for the purpose of getting to know the creatures He has created.

As God called forth the Israelite nation as the covenant people, He enjoined on them the Ten Commandments—not as arbitrary restrictions, but as a way of life for redeemed people. That's why He prefaced the giving of the law with these words:

> And God spake all these words, saying, I am the LORD thy God, which have brought thee out of the land of Egypt, out of the house of bondage. (Exodus 20:1, 2.)

The law was not given as an obligation, but as a guide to a redeemed people. The law was never given to a people in bondage—only to a people already redeemed by God. Yet in their humanity they could not keep the sacred law; they needed a divine relationship to enable them to live a life in harmony with the Ten Commandments. So in the very heart of the commandments God inserted a command that dealt with the relationship with God. God knew that only by keeping the fourth commandment and developing a relationship with Him would it be possible for His people to keep the other nine commandments. Note the wording of this commandment:

> "Remember the sabbath day, to keep it holy. Six days shalt thou labour, and do all thy work: but the seventh day is the sabbath of the LORD thy

God: in it thou shalt not do any work, thou, nor
thy son, nor thy daughter, thy manservant, nor
thy maidservant, nor thy cattle, nor thy stranger
that is within thy gates: For in six days the LORD
made heaven and earth, the sea, and all that in
them is, and rested the seventh day: wherefore
the Lord blessed the sabbath day, and hallowed
it. (Exodus 20:8-11.)

Note that God refers Israel back to the creation
experience for the origin of this special day. As
God calls the nation of Israel into existence, He
informs them of the great necessity to devote one
day a week exclusively to building a relationship
with Him. The restrictions were not placed on this
day because God is arbitrary, but to challenge
people not to allow anything to interfere with their
relationship with Him on this day.

Some people feel that they do not need to keep
the Sabbath today. They feel that it is a relic of the
Jewish age, even though the origin of the Sabbath
is at creation, not Sinai. Somehow they feel they
can get along with just daily time with God. Remember, God has not left this choice to us. He has
already decided that we need this time with Him.
Do we know better than God does? It is He who
set aside the Sabbath in the beginning; it is He who
commanded it to His redeemed people in the Ten
Commandments; it is He who wants this time with
us to develop a deep relationship.

The last days of human history demand the deep-
est relationship with God that mankind has ever
experienced. If mankind needed a day with God
in the perfect Paradise of Eden, then how much
greater is our need for this time with God today,
given the hectic pace of modern life? As we near

the end of time, Sabbath keeping becomes even more critical for God's people, because there is a greater need for a relationship.

Not only did Jesus keep the Sabbath when on earth (Luke 4:16), He commanded His followers to keep it after His death (Matthew 24:20). It was the custom of the apostle Paul and all the apostles of Jesus to regularly keep God's Sabbath as they inaugurated Christianity in the world (Acts 13:14, 42-44; 16:13; 17:1-4; 18:1-4). For nearly 400 years after the death of Christ, the early church continued to keep the seventh-day Sabbath on Saturday each week. They spent that whole day building a relationship with God. As the little horn power came into existence and gained increasing power, Sabbath keeping disappeared.

Satan tempted the church of the Dark Ages to change the Sabbath from Saturday to Sunday so that people would forget about the need of a deep relationship with God. Amazingly, as this power gained the ascendancy, people's spirituality decreased. Soon the Bible was withheld from the people, and the populace was told they could not understand the Scriptures except through the church.

As we near the end of time, it is important that the great Sabbath truth once again be restored to the church. This is not the legalistic keeping of a day, but rather the keeping of a special moment in time in order to maintain a relationship with God, just as in Eden. This is a bulwark against the final king of the north, who is soon to gain full control of the world. The only ones who will stand in that crisis hour are those who have a deep, abiding relationship with Jesus. Such a relationship can be gained only by daily Bible study and prayer and by weekly Sabbath keeping.

This is why the Sabbath is one of the crucial issues in last-day events. The remnant who are ready to meet Jesus are ready only because they have taken adequate time to build this solid relationship. They not only have a daily time with God, but they also keep God's Sabbath for the purpose of intensifying the relationship. Theirs is not a legalistic obedience, springing out of obligation, but a loving experience developed out of the need for a deep, abiding relationship. Many people who perhaps are keeping the Sabbath legalistically will be swept away by the deceptions of the last days. If a person does not use this time to build his/her relationship with God, it is a waste of time to keep the Sabbath at all.

In Revelation God clearly identifies those whom the beast, or king of the north, is seeking to destroy. They are the remnant, who keep the commandments of God and have the testimony of Jesus Christ (Revelation 12:17). Why is the devil so angry with these people? Because they keep the commandments, including the one which enables them to keep all the others—the Sabbath, the commandment delineating the need for a relationship with God.

That's why the Sabbath is the deciding issue in the final events. The greatest need of the last days is to have a relationship with God, and the remnant have discovered the necessary ingredients for that relationship. They realize they must use the Sabbath that God has commanded to build a relationship with Him.

If you would like to know more about the Sabbath—if you would like to know how to keep this special day to build a relationship with God—write to the publisher of this book and ask for further information about God's seventh-day Sabbath.

Yes, history is racing toward the climax of the ages. The sky is about to open, and our Lord will descend in majesty. Are you ready? You can be if you have accepted Jesus as Lord of your life. Having done that, you need to begin to deepen that relationship through regular Bible study, prayer, and weekly Sabbath keeping. Then you too will rejoice in the blessed hope of the glorious and soon appearing of the Lord Jesus Christ.

Maranatha! Come quickly, Lord Jesus. Amen.

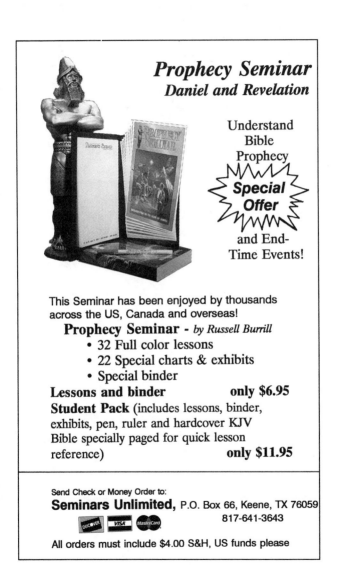